Is something keeping you from your creative dreams?

Wake up to the way your fear is holding back your creative potential.

Shake up your limiting beliefs with a new way of thinking about failure.

Make up with yourself by softening toward your creative anxiety. And

GO!

Written on Gunditjmara land

Published 2023

Cover and book design by Buzzy Lewis

Printed in Australia by IngramSpark

Page layout design by Dawn Black

Edited by Kevin Miller (www.kevinmillerxi.com)

Library of Congress Cataloging-in-Publication Data is available from the National Library of Australia

Printed book: ISBN 978-0-6452519-1-3

E-book: ISBN 978-0-6452519-2-0

Author: Bethany (Buzzy) Lewis

Title: Failure Friendly

Failurefriendly.com

@failure_friendly

All Inquiries: Buzzy Lewis, buzzy@failurefriendly.com

TABLE OF CONTENTS

I dedicate this book

To all the failures that have gotten me to where I am today.

KEYWORDS AND DEFINITIONS

The Failure Friendly Mindset: Choosing to Transcend Creative Anxiety

Being **Failure Friendly** is accepting that fear is a part of life and an important part of the creative process. It is not something you need to stop or reject, just something you need to understand. It has a very important role in letting you know when you are trying something new and entering uncertain terrain. But fear does not get to make the decisions. Fear's decision will always be 'no' or 'stop'. When it comes to your creative pursuits, the stakes are rarely life or death, the answer should always be 'yes' and 'go'.

Perception refers to how we interpret and understand things based on the information gathered by our senses. It is possible to alter our perceptions. Instead of perceiving only hopelessness and setbacks, you can seek a new way of looking at your situation. In the spiritual text *A Course of Miracles*, this shift of perception is referred to as a 'miracle'.

Mindset encompasses a set of established attitudes held by an individual. Our mindset shapes and influences our perceptions and therefore our reality, and choices.

For instance, imagine two people with different mindsets, waiting at the airport to board the same plane, both eager to return home. Unexpectedly, their flight gets canceled. The first person holds a mindset fixated on control, becomes angry, and feels helpless. He has no choice but to wait hours for the next flight. The second man has a growth mindset. Sure, the cancellation is frustrating for him too but instead of feeling helpless he feels inspired and begins looking for a way to solve his problem. He starts talking to people. He hires a plane, a pilot and a blackboard. He advertises the replacement flight on the blackboard to his fellow passengers whose flight has been cancelled, sells tickets to cover the hire fees and flies home. He is Richard Brandon, and this is how Virgin Airlines was born.

Choice. Ultimately, it comes down to choice. This book isn't about controlling your life, thoughts, or fears. We have less control over these things than we would like to admit. Instead, we have agency over the meaning and power we give to events or fearful thoughts. This agency lets us change our perspective, our mindset and our reality.

Transcending implies going beyond your perceived limits. This book is not about destroying fear but gently moving beyond fear and not allowing it to hold us back.

Creative Anxiety is a psychological obstacle to creativity — a paralyzing feeling of unease, worry or nervousness while engaging in the creative process. The symptoms it causes can be physical, such as shakiness and a racing heart, and at its worst, it can take away our ability to create.

Warning:

You've picked this book because you want to reach your creative potential. Whether you want to work in a creative industry or create your own job, you wish to lead a fulfilling and vibrantly creative life. There's a 'but' coming. *But* you're frustrated with that invisible barrier that has been holding you back, and everything that you have tried so far hasn't worked.

This book asks you to suspend the beliefs that have not been serving you and to try on new ways of thinking. Many of the lessons in this book can feel counterintuitive, asking you to embrace paradoxes that seem contradictory. Some will be easy to adopt while others may challenge your core beliefs. Like a child wrapped tightly around their parent's leg, you may find yourself resistant to change.

Trying on new ideas doesn't mean you have to buy into them. If they don't fit, you can always go back to your old ones. If you're feeling stressed, hopeless or out of control at the moment, then your current strategy is not working. So, why not give this one a try? The worst case is that you will know that this isn't for you. The best case is freedom. A transformed mindset that is robust, courageous, productive and unapologetically you!

It's worth it.

1
WAKE UP

The things no one told me about fear, failure and creativity

HOW DID I GET HERE?

In this book are the things I wish I could have told my younger self. All I wanted to do was bring my ideas to life, but my innocence led me down many painful roads, resulting in hurts that I carried with me for years. The lessons in this book have healed those wounds, and now I am proud of my scars.

I was a happy, imaginative child who loved to draw and paint. At school I learned that I was a good drawer and a poor student. Looking back, it seems I might have some form of undiagnosed dyslexia. It took me a painfully long time to tell the time, read, spell and to get numbers in the right order. Even now when I read aloud, I confuse people by missing crucial words or letters. And my handwriting is an intentional scrawl to disguise the letters I accidentally skip over. I am a visual learner. To understand information I need to break it down and reorganize it into diagrams, flowcharts or stories. This is how I functioned, in secret. I was ashamed that I didn't think like everyone else, that I couldn't just read slabs of text and make sense of it. I knew that something was wrong with me, that I just wasn't good enough, but at least I could draw.

It wasn't until year twelve when I attended an exam preparation workshop that I heard experts introduce revolutionary techniques that would allow us to remember so much more. The same visual techniques I had been hiding for twelve years, my classmates were now lapping up. In this bizarre experience, I caught a glimpse of my 'flaws' for what they actually are: my greatest strengths.

During my graphic design course at university, I only ever took one exam, for a marketing elective. In preparation for the exam, I embraced my visual thinking and made huge, colourful flowcharts. By understanding the relationship between all the different psychological theories, I understood how they all fit together, making them easy to recall. I received an award that year for the highest mark in the marketing class, even out of the marketing students. It was nice to have a smart person award, but I told myself that must have been luck. I still couldn't shake the belief that I was just a dumb person who could draw.

I decided I wasn't good enough to be a designer after my first freelance client. I got so freaked out about doing a simple business card. I hesitated and procrastinated and missed the deadline by a week. I felt so bad about it that I wouldn't let them pay me. So, I went back to painting. After posting a photo of a painting on Facebook, I accidentally made my first sale and then took orders for a few commissions. My parents helped me rent an art studio, and just like that, I was an artist! It was fun—until I realized I didn't know how to be an artist and that I probably I wasn't good enough to be one. Eventually, I couldn't step inside the studio. I felt so guilty for wasting such an amazing opportunity. Next, I did what I thought all failed artists do: I became an art teacher. In the classroom I found that I didn't have the confidence to lead a class. I was so frustrated by the many students who were so anxious about making a mistake that they refused to engage. I knew their pain intimately, and I was not the role model they needed.

After that failure I hit rock bottom. What was the point of living if I couldn't do the one thing I wanted to do: make the big ideas that

I saw in my head a reality? It seemed like no matter what, my lack of confidence always got in my way. I was a prisoner of my own mind and a spectator to my own life.

Right when I decided I would give up, light pierced the darkness with a surprising thought: 'Figure it out'. Thanks to this invitation, from rock bottom I began to figure out creativity and anxiety. Books came to me, and they all seemed to have the next nugget of wisdom I needed. I started to document the lessons, so I wouldn't forget them. I first gathered these lessons into the 'Failure Friendly Classroom' eBook (which you can download for free at www.failurefriendly.com). As I put them into practice, interesting things started to happen. I had the confidence to ask for a job at a great design firm and even landed a job as the marketing manager at a beauty company. I wrote a thesis, got a Masters degree, I travelled overseas, I started selling my art, I became an entrepreneur, I launched a website, I started my own design agency and I bought another business, all within two years. Things that seemed impossible to me only a few years ago are now part of my everyday life, which gives me confidence that the goals that seem out of reach now are possible too.

Thanks to the toolkit I have gathered into this book, if I have an idea today, I know I have the skills and the resources to go for it. This book is also a reminder to keep practicing these lessons daily. It is all too easy to fall back into old thinking habits and forget the way. But don't worry; becoming failure friendly isn't about being perfect. It's about knowing how to return to a healthier approach when we inevitably slip.

TO FLY YOU HAVE TO TRUST YOUR WINGS

We cannot live life to the full when only half of us is showing up. When you suppress your creative calling, you suppress yourself. When you're scared of making mistakes, of what other people might think or of being wrong, you stop taking creative risks. You stop being you.

It's not your fault. Our society has labelled creative expression as different, difficult and weird. It's something society accepts but doesn't understand. When creativity results in products or services that make lives better, it's praised. But the mainstream doesn't want to talk about the 'dark side', the torment artists experience on the roller coaster that is the creative process.

Because of this strange positioning, many of us turn our back on our creativity because we don't trust it. It's too unpredictable, too intense, unlike anything we have been prepared for. Why couldn't we just be normal? When we treat this natural part of us with such contempt, we disown a huge part of ourselves.

This book is not trying to address a fear of making mistakes; it's addressing the fear of being different, weird and not being accepted for who you really are. Your creativity is your wings. It's your gift, your unique and valuable voice. Can you hear it calling your name?

SAY HELLO TO FEAR

Fear plays a vital role in our survival by alerting us to and protecting us from danger. If it weren't for the amygdala in our brain that produces fear, our ancestors would have fallen prey to wild animals, the weather or each other. The thing is, like our school systems, which are struggling to keep up with the changing world, our brains are still working on outdated software. Our lizard brain still thinks we're under threat of extinction.

So, our brains read anything that is new and uncertain, even if it's as safe as a blank page, in the same way as if it were a dark gorilla lurking jungle. Cue stress response, adrenaline, heart pounding, hands sweating and that tight, uncomfortable feeling of your body on edge. For a long time we have accepted that there are three traditional responses to fear: fight, flight or freeze. In this book I offer two further options to meet your fear as a friend or as a leader. But first, let's understand where fear comes from.

FEAR IS CONTAGIOUS

Do you know that humans are only born with two innate fears? The fear of falling and the fear of loud noises. All other fears—spiders, the dark, heights, failure—are learned. Michael Cook at the University of Wisconsin discovered that monkeys who have never been afraid of snakes quickly learn to be frightened of them if they see that another monkey is scared. And it only has to happen once.

We learn fear from our role models and the people around us. We also learn confidence this way, which is why it's so important to choose your company wisely. Find role models and communities of people who have done what you want to do. Read their books, listen to their podcasts, watch their videos and lean into their circles. It's said that you become the people you spend the most time with, so hang out with your heroes.

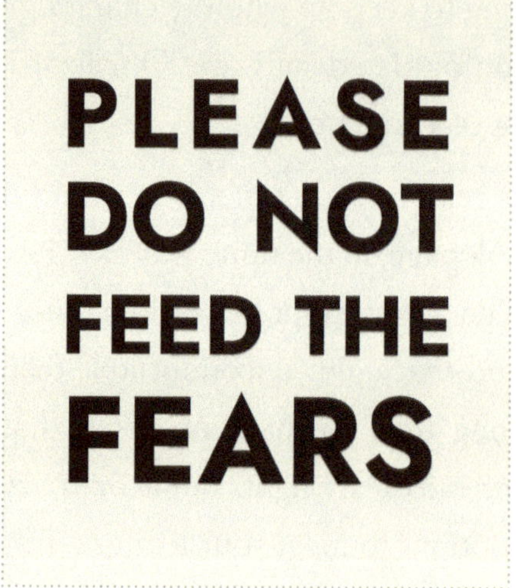

ANXIETY IS PART OF ANY CREATIVE PROCESS

The rules for creativity break all of the rules we are taught to obey in school. By definition, creativity is going into the unknown and relinquishing control while paradoxically making choices. All of these things produce anxiety on a physiological level. 'Creative anxiety' is not a condition; it's a natural phenomenon. There is no guarantee that we will succeed in our creative endeavours, and this produces anxiety. The thought of sharing our work with others to judge produces anxiety. Making mistakes produces anxiety. However, research shows that creativity not only likes mistakes, it needs them.

There is no way to avoid anxiety when it comes to creativity, so we need to accept that it is part of the process. When we accept it we can prepare for it. (That's what this book is all about!)

FAILING SAFELY

To enter the creative arena we must be ready to fail in order to succeed. Accepting that failure is better than not trying at all is the only way to live a regret-free life. But if you invest your whole life savings blindly into your creative project without leaving room for a safety net, you are not being brave; you are being reckless.

Potentially setting yourself up for bigger failures is not necessary. Being creatively courageous involves choosing to take risks, but more accurately, choosing which risks to take. Minimizing the risk with a backup plan and an awareness of the landscape, the players and the changing conditions, as well as choosing to 'test before you invest', will make success more likely and failure more manageable.

TIP: Want to turn your creativity into a business? Test your assumptions and ideas quickly and cheaply before you invest by learning about the Lean Startup Movement and Design Thinking Methodology, learn more at theleanstartup.com

WHY IS IT SO EASY TO FEEL LIKE A FAILURE?

Failure is the opposite of success, which is accomplishing an aim or purpose. So, before we can deem something as unsuccessful or a 'failure' we must be clear about the aim. In the classroom or studio the aim is not to produce perfect pieces of work in the first attempt—or any attempt, for that matter. The aim is to learn, grow and progress.

When I had my first art studio, my only goal was to prove myself. I would tell myself over and over, 'This is my chance; prove that I have some artistic talent. Quickly!' Looking back it's unsurprising why I choked. I had no clear, tangible goals, no vision of what 'proof' would be—or failure, for that matter. So, no matter what I did achieve, no matter how valuable, it was never enough to satisfy the impossible goal. Unknowingly, I set myself up to fail.

The second time around (three years later) my goal was simply to create every time I was in the studio. It didn't have to be good, and I didn't have to share it with anyone; I just had to make something. Failure would have been sitting there in the studio trolling social media or twiddling my thumbs.

Being clear about what I needed to achieve, I was able to put safety nets in place for when the creative juices were not flowing. It was as simple as having a box of magazines and a scalpel. To keep me creating I would make simple collages that required little thought. I had fun the second time around, and I made some work I'm really proud of, especially those collages!

TIP: When starting a project, get clear on your definition of success and failure. Write them down. It must be something that you can control and track; otherwise, you have no way of knowing if you've succeeded.

FAILURE FRIENDLY

"Failure Friendly," two words that don't normally sit side by side. The word 'failure' elicits constrictive feelings of dread. As you read it, you probably held your breath. When you read 'Friendly', on the other hand, you most likely loosened up a little and maybe even smiled. So, why am I asking you to pair these opposing ideas?

There is nothing wrong with the word 'failure'; the problem is the meaning we attach to it. We are taught that failure is bad and to avoid it at all costs. Schools, with their focus on testing, condition us to search for 'the one' right answer instead of seeing that in life, there is more than one solution to any problem. To fail is to be wrong, and naturally, we desire to be accepted, so we can belong. This fear is ancient, from a time when belonging to a group or not was the difference between survival and extinction.

The problem is that we attach our success and failure to our sense of self, to our identity. If I fail, I am a failure. If I succeed, I am a success. It's too much pressure with too much is on the line. And it's not true. Failure is just a lesson. It's the key to success, and it has nothing to do with who you are or your worth in the world. It's time to make friends with failure and the fear it produces.

FEARLESS OR FEAR-LESS

Ever wished you were fearless? The word 'fearless' means 'showing a lack of fear'. The word 'lack' denotes 'not having enough of something'. Fearlessness, by definition, is an insufficient amount of fear. A life without fear is the life of an unhappy psychopath.

Studies consistently show that people with an inability to feel fear go to extreme lengths to feel anything. In many cases they become serial killers. Trust me, you do not want to have zero fear.

Although the idea of wishing away your anxieties may seem ideal, you would be wishing away your happiness along with it. Fear and excitement are two sides of the same coin. You can't have one without the other. This book does not promise to make you fearless; instead it will allow you to fear less. You will always have fear, but you don't have to fear your fear. You will learn to take your fear by the hand and say, 'I feel fear, but I'm doing this anyway'. This may not sound very enticing right now, but as you get more and more comfortable with your fear you will begin to see it in a new light.

It has been said that fear is just excitement without the breath. So, the next time you feel fear, take a deep breath, and feel the excitement of doing something new! We will delve into transforming fear into excitement in more depth soon, but what I want you to try and accept right now is that fear is fabulous! Love your fear because in it lies the answers to living your most exciting life. It won't be clear yet, but the first step is to be open to seeing fear differently.

FEAR CAN WORK FOR YOU

When I signed up to do my first art market, I didn't know what I was doing, but I was committed to it and rose to the challenge. As the market date loomed closer, I began to panic and live in a state of worry. My head swirled with questions motivated by fear: 'What if my stand looks unprofessional?', 'What if I don't have enough stock', 'How will I transport it all?', 'How long will it take to get set up?',

'What if I don't allow myself enough time?' I was freaking out. Then I thought, hey, I can do something about this. I'm worrying about these things because they are legitimate concerns. But worrying about them doesn't help me. I have to turn this worry into action and planning.

In flipping this switch, I realised I could practice setting up my market stand to see where the gaps were, and I could pack it all beforehand, so I knew it was done. By saying, 'Hey this is important. What can I do about it right now? How can I help myself right now?', I was able to pull myself out of worry. I returned from the future to the present moment where I could take action. If it wasn't for the fear and worry, I wouldn't have been so organised and productive. I would have turned up at the market two hours late without half of the things I needed, and I probably wouldn't have sold any art.

On the day of that first market, I felt relaxed and grateful knowing that I had done so much preparation. All I needed to do was show up and do the thing. I was actually a little too relaxed, lost track of time and arrived when the market opened rather than beforehand. While early customers walked around, I was still struggling to set up my marquee. Fear said, 'OMG you look so unprofessional right now. You are such a noob!'

'Next time I will get here way earlier because I do feel a bit silly', I replied, 'but cut me some slack. I've worked hard. Even if I'm a bit late this is going to be fun'.

Fear can work for you. It's your security team that alerts you to potential threats. It sounds the alarm by producing worry. It's then your job to transform from worrier to warrior by taking action or devising a plan to deal with the threats.

FEAR-LESS TO FAITH-FULL

Ever tried a crash diet to stop an unhealthy eating habit? Depriving yourself of junk food altogether to find yourself hating every moment of it? Starting a cycle of self-hate: depriving, bingeing, punishing yourself with more bingeing and then punishing your bingeing with starvation? On and on it goes, with the unhealthy eating habit becoming even stronger.

How about an add-in diet? You eat whatever you normally do and just 'add-in' some extra healthy whole foods, fruits or veggies. The more you eat wholesome goodies, the more you realise they satisfy you so much more. Eventually, the sugary foods fall away. You begin to see eating well as giving to yourself rather than taking away.

It's the same with fear. Rather than focusing on removing the nasty fears (which is impossible), focus on adding in more trust, faith and empathy. Soon your mind will see which mindset serves you better, and it will crave those positive thinking patterns. Given the choice of 'You have to do this; it should have been done weeks ago!' or 'I can do this!', which do you think fuels your creativity most effectively?

Becoming fear-less is actually about becoming faith-full. Having a healthy dose of faith in yourself, your resourcefulness, skills and abilities is the easiest way to face the twists and turns of creative life. The resources that follow all help in restoring a healthy balance of faith, self-worth and positive thinking that has been lacking in your fear focused mind.

UNLEARNING FEAR

While fear is a part of life, we can reduce the hold it has on us by unlearning it. The process put forward in this book to unlearn your creativity crushing fears is based on Guided Mastery and Exposure Therapy, two psychological strategies used to overcome extreme fears and phobias. The key principles taken from these test strategies are:

- Using a progression of steps toward the fear stimulus (baby steps)

- Minimizing the time between exposures of the fear stimulus (avoiding fear makes it stronger)

- Learning new relationships to the fear stimulus (a new way to look at it and yourself)

THE GROWTH MINDSET

Our mind has a set of established attitudes and beliefs that guide our reality, our perceptions and choices. We call this our 'mindset'. Stanford University professor Carol Dweck's research has shown that humans have one of two mindsets: a fixed mindset or a growth mindset.

Someone with a fixed mindset thinks that natural talent is more important than effort, as if they have no control over their achievements. When faced with an error or failure, they think things like 'Well, I can't do it. I'm not good enough. I need to cheat next time, and I need to find someone worse than me to make me feel better'. When they succeed, they credit luck rather than skill.

Someone with a growth mindset meets errors with excitement and thoughts like 'I'm not there yet. What have I learned from this? How can I do it better next time? There must be a way! I love challenges.'

People with fixed mindsets feel powerless when it comes to challenges. They run from difficulty. People with growth mindsets are nobody's victim. They use mistakes to make them better, not bitter.

> *Don't run from mistakes; learn from them*

Wouldn't it be great to have a growth mindset? Dweck's research goes on to explain how parents, teachers and other individuals can foster such a positive outlook. Simply by praising wisely, commending things that you or your child can control like perseverance, process or effort.

By detaching from talent we instantly become more resilient in the face of challenges. As creatives we have most likely received feedback for our work from people who don't understand it. 'You're so talented', 'You're a genius', 'So naturally gifted' or worse 'That isn't what it should look like' or 'You're not one of the gifted ones'. Compliments feel great until you believe them. When you believe your own 'talent', it turns failures along the way into dead ends. 'I can't even do this. My talent mustn't be that great. Maybe I was a fool to think I was talented in the first place'.

Praising talent or intelligence, things we don't have control over, makes us believe we are special but not in control. Being special doesn't help you overcome dead-ends. But believing in your power no matter what challenges you face turns dead-ends into springboards to grow, to become better, stronger and wiser.

Meanwhile, criticism for your lack of talent, without constructive feedback, will have you running from creative challenges for the rest of your life. In one of the most popular TED Talks of all time, Sir Ken Robinson struck a nerve when he shared the way so many of us can be robbed of creative joy with just a handful of critical words.

Choose growth. See errors, mistakes and failures as temporary, a sign that you're not there yet. Embrace your power to learn, grow and improve so that your life and creative work is more enjoyable and productive. 'But I just can't', I hear the fixed-mindset people say. 'I don't know how'. That is what this book is all about. When you embrace your power, you embrace the problem-solving part of your brain that will find the 'how'.

WHEN YOU CHANGE THE WAY YOU LOOK AT THINGS, THE THINGS YOU LOOK AT CHANGE

The growth mindset harnesses the power of the mind to change the way you see obstacles. This is just the beginning of using your mind for good instead of evil. Your mind is a powerful tool that I like to think of as a magnet. It takes effort to charge your mind magnet in the direction you want, positive or negative. But once you've set your intention, it does the work for you, finding solutions in new perspectives.

We've all been around negative people who think negative thoughts, have negative energy and attract negative experiences. Just like the negative pole of a magnet, they repel good people and opportunities. The opposite is true of positive people. They attract more positivity. When you get to know someone who seems to have the best of everything, you soon realize they don't; they just make the best of everything. When they hit obstacles and make mistakes, they just choose not to dwell on them.

Depending on your social circles, positive people can seem harder to come by. This is because, thanks to education, politics and advertising, our culture is dominated by negative or fear-based thinking. We are trained to believe we need to compete to get ahead, that other people should be treated as a threat. Fear sells. Fear gets votes. Fear controls. But love wins.

A thought system based on love rather than fear says that, like the millions of cells in the body, we as society are all connected and working together for the greater good. We all have a unique and valuable role to play. Love and positivity are our natural and healthy state of being. When fear and negativity enter the party, we begin to attack ourselves which limits our potential and eventually weakens society as a whole. The same way certain cells can start to reject or work against each other, attacking the health of the body the cells live in, cancer is born.

Biologist Bruce Lipton, founder of the revolutionary science of epigenetics, discovered that, contrary to what scientists thought, your genetics are not your destiny. Genes can be changed. This is great news if you are hoping to change any aspect of your life.

Lipton found that cells changed not just due to their DNA but also because of their environment. The environment cells live in is our blood. Healthy blood means positive growth, and unhealthy blood means negative mutations.

There are two ways to influence the condition of your blood and, therefore, your cells. The first is your thoughts and the second way is through your diet.

Thoughts are electricity in the brain that result in hormones being pumped into your blood. Here's an example.

Thought: 'I have so much to do. I'm never going to get through this in time. I'm doomed!'

Hormone: Cortisol, the stress hormone, is released into the blood.

Result: Havoc on your cells, constriction in the body, and an inability to focus = creative block

Or, Thought: 'Look how much I've already achieved. It's amazing what I can accomplish!'

Hormone: Dopamine, the feel-good hormone, is released into the blood.

Result: Increased focus, energy and drive = productivity

Being positive is not wishy-washy or woo-woo. Science proves that choosing to think positively in a thought system based in love is better for your health, wealth and happiness.

Negative thinking is corrosive to your health; it's insanity to prefer it!

The second way we can directly affect the condition of our blood (the home of our cells) is the nutrients we put into our body: food.

I like to remember that 'food that grows will make you grow'. So, foods fuelled by the sun (fruit, veggies and whole grains) are what you want to put into your body.

Foods that do not grow from the ground and are instead made in factories will contain artificial colouring, sweeteners and preservatives. Once swallowed, these chemicals turn into sugar. Sugar, a.k.a. the 'legal drug' then stimulates your appetite and makes you hungrier, meaning the more you eat, the emptier you will feel. It also releases a stress response in the body, leading to lack of focus, quickened, shallow breathing and after a burst of scattered energy, leaves you totally zapped. In the long term, sugar is as addictive as cocaine and leads to a plethora of deadly preventable diseases.

So, while you harness the power of positive thinking, remember to give that powerful brain of yours the fuel it needs.

A SIDE NOTE ON DIET

By fearing certain foods, you give them power over you. It is not about depriving yourself of the delicious sugar; it's about *giving* yourself delicious energy to accomplish your dreams. Try not to deprive or limit yourself from anything.

I'm a chocoholic, so take everything I say with a grain of salt. The only way I have ever quit sugar (the legal drug) was not by focusing on cutting it out but instead adding in more nutrients. Combining a piece of sweet fruit, a soothing cup of tea or a huge gulp of water with your poison of choice will make you feel better. Eventually, you will rush back for the strawberries instead of the strawberry-flavoured milk.

When you can eat whatever you want guilt free, after the initial splurge, you will choose the food that nourishes you rather than depletes you. It's the same with healthy thoughts!

THIS A JOURNEY; GET A JOURNAL

This book asks you to use the power of your thoughts to change the way you see fear and failure. It's a theory that only works if you allow yourself to participate. Give yourself the best chance by starting a Failure Friendly journal to complete the exercises in this book and track your progress.

It's like the funny dream or the phone message you're convinced you'll remember, so you don't write it down. Then, boom, it's gone, the details wiped from your memory forever!

These lessons have a better chance of sticking if you write them down. Get your value for your money and time by doing the self-reflections and the exercises along the way.

Journalling will show you that you are your own best teacher. Your guru is waiting for you in the pages of your journal; I promise.

2
SHAKE UP

It's time to turn fear into excitement, your mistakes into discoveries, your challenges into experiments and your worries into action. Are you ready to try a new way of thinking?

THE FAILURE FRIENDLY MINDSET

The Failure Friendly Mindset is the antidote for a fixed and fearful mind that strangles creativity in its overly critical beliefs.

A pressure cooker is no place for creativity to thrive, so the Failure Friendly Mindset addresses the external environment (the classroom or creative space) and the internal environment (the mind) as each affects the other.

It is of utmost importance to feel safe in your space and around others but more importantly within yourself. To be creative you must grant yourself permission to take risks and make mistakes. Both produce anxiety, and within both lies the magic.

The aim of the Failure Friendly Mindset is resilience, confidence and a sense of agency. You will hit obstacles, you will fall down and you will feel scared, but you will come out the other side. You will learn to invite uncertainty, chase mistakes and appreciate the struggle. You will harness the power of your magnetic mind to transform obstacles into opportunities, breakdowns into breakthroughs and the rock bottom into rock 'n' roll.

Creative living is an exciting life with extreme ups and downs. The difference that the Failure Friendly Mindset makes is that you will see both for what they are: temporary. With confidence in yourself, you will enjoy the ups and move gracefully through the downs, emerging stronger than before.

You were put on this planet to create. Trust in who you are and what you have to offer. Embrace that it will never be perfect and that it's a process. Show up fully as your true self, and never pretend you're normal. You are exceptional.

GUIDING PRINCIPLES

BELIEFS

The following core beliefs are at the centre of the Failure Friendly Mindset.

Creative skill is flexible, not fixed

Your creative and artistic skills are flexible rather than fixed from birth. You are in control of your ability to learn, grow and progress toward your dreams.

Creativity is an essential skill for everyone

The world is facing a 'creative crisis'. The majority of students today will work in jobs that have not yet been created. In a world of increasingly rapid change, individuals must be innovative and create their own jobs by embracing their natural creativity.

Fear and excitement are two sides of the same coin

Within fear lies the secret to living your most exciting creative life. Don't run from your fear; move toward it.

VALUES

The following values should guide your creative path, helping you make choices that serve you and your creative dreams. Display them in your creative space to keep you moving in the right direction.

Mistakes are Discoveries

Discoveries (often mistaken for mistakes) are a necessary part of the learning and creative process. Aim to fail fast by presenting yourself with 'manageable failures' that you can deal with and learn from. The goal is to grow, not to be perfect the first time.

Risk Taking

When the goal is to create something completely new, risk taking is rewarded and essential. Challenging yourself shows that you believe in yourself and builds confidence. Set tasks that scare you and then rise to the challenge.

Empathy/Friendliness

There is no room for judgment, criticism, shame or blame in the Failure Friendly Mindset. To be able to take risks you need a high level of emotional support and a deep sense of security. Within your team and within yourself, always act and talk with kindness and understanding.

Playfulness

Play is the biggest driver for innovation. It can unlock new ideas, new possibilities and creative confidence. Fear cannot drive when you are being playful, so give yourself permission to play!

The Journey, not the Destination

If you live in the future or the past, you will never feel like you can cope because you can't make a difference in either. You can only act now in the present. Anchor yourself in the present moment. In a creative project it is easy to pin your happiness on the finished product. If you focus on the destination, you will miss the adventure. We never arrive; our goalposts are constantly moving, which keeps the journey exciting and challenging.

Purpose

Ask yourself what you want to achieve and then ask yourself why. The answer is your purpose, your intrinsic motivation and your compass. External motivators like money, societal expectations and stereotypes will drag you off course. Check in with your purpose on your creative journey regularly and then adjust your course if necessary. Don't be fooled by external forces that tell us the end result or the financial reward is the prize, creative people are motivated by the creative process itself.

RULES

Rules are necessary in a creative environment because they make us feel safe and secure, so uphold them consistently.

Accept You

Creative spaces don't judge. Everybody's free to express themselves; we accept and support each other without judgment. It's most important to accept yourself not for your talent, accomplishments or possessions but for who you are. No judgments allowed.

Watch Your Language

To stay resilient in the face of creative anxiety, we must listen to what we are saying to ourselves, actively choose positive affirmations and useful self-talk. Instead of agreeing with your nasty inner critic, choose language that propels you. Name-calling, blame and shame are off limits.

Go Wild

Wild ideas can often give rise to creative leaps. In thinking about ideas that are wacky or 'out there', we tend to think about what we really want without the constraints of technology or materials. Then we can take those magical possibilities and perhaps invent new technologies to deliver them.

The More the Merrier

Aim to generate as many new ideas as possible. At IDEO, the design thinking firm, they've proven that up to one hundred ideas can be generated in sixty minutes. I didn't say one hundred amazing ideas - out of ten ideas one might be worth exploring, but you don't get to that idea without the nine stepping stone ideas that came before. Crank the ideas out quickly, no time for analysis. This is about giving yourself more choices, so don't worry about being wrong. The person who has made the most mistakes has usually learned the most.

Keep It Constructive

When making decisions and giving feedback, only praise and critique things that are within your control. Thinking you're a genius or a failure isn't helpful. Focus on technique and persistence, the process, emphasizing progress and growth. It's much easier to be motivated when you believe you're in control.

Note: You can download printable and interactive resources like the guiding principles at www.failurefriendly.com

THE CREATIVE JOURNEY

DISCOVERIES

I was going to call this section 'Allow Yourself to Make Mistakes', but then I realised that there are no mistakes in the Failure Friendly Mindset, only discoveries. A mistake is an act that is judged as wrong or incorrect. When it comes to the creative process, it's called a 'process' for a reason. It's a series of actions or steps taken to achieve a particular end (a creation of some sort). When an action step doesn't turn out the way you hoped, you can call this a 'mistake' or 'failure'. But by labelling it this way, you put yourself in the wrong and erode your self-esteem, which often leads to disengagement from the process altogether. Alternatively, you can do as scientists do and turn it into an experiment. An experiment is a scientific procedure undertaken to make a discovery, test a hypothesis or demonstrate a known fact. Experiments don't aim to be right or wrong; their only goal is to learn something. If you approach your creative process with the same attitude, your 'discoveries' will not slow you down. So, your watercolour bleeds into an area you didn't mean it to, or you hit a note that wasn't on the sheet music; what have you learned? What does it mean? How did it happen? How can you use this to guide future experiments? What can you do to stop this from happening or increase the probability of it happening next time? (See how your curiosity is sparked by 'discoveries'?)

Failure Friendly creatives like prolific inventor Thomas Edison embrace their discoveries to invent life-changing creations. Edison said, 'I have not failed. I've just found 10,000 ways that won't work'. Mistakes slam doors. Discoveries open the sky of possibilities. Even if you take pride in having high standards (like I do) and believe your art can be right or wrong, good enough or not good enough (like I'm trying to stop doing), you have to admit that mistakes are disappointing. Discoveries are exciting. The actions are the same, but the thinking is different. Why choose to feel downtrodden when you can feel energised and inspired?

I used to take pride in the fact that I was a perfectionist. I had high standards; I would never put out work that I wasn't proud of, but I was also never satisfied. No matter how good it was, it was never good enough, never perfect. Just as expecting they're to be no mistakes on your journey is misguided, expecting the result to be 'perfect' is insane. It sets you up for failure. Perfectionism is the fear of never being enough. If you suffer from perfectionism, I urge you to see that you are enough and that 'done is better than perfect'.

ACTION BOX

In one column list all the big failures or mistakes you have made in your life. In the next column write the lessons you have learned from them and why you are glad you made those discoveries.

A CALM SEA NEVER MADE A SKILLED SAILOR

Humans are incapable of predicting everything that will happen in the future; therefore, obstacles and hiccups are an inevitable part of life. By expecting the journey to run smoothly and fearing obstacles along the way, we are setting ourselves up for failure and a dream-crushing reality.

What do you do when you hit bumps in the road? I have been known to be very short tempered when it comes to technology not doing what I want. After a while I would give myself two options: give up or change the goal to be more attainable. Am I giving up on my goal? Perhaps but it's justified because what I wanted to achieve is impossible. That's acceptable right?

Wrong! Did Nelson Mandela say, 'Goodbye dream', when he hit obstacles after obstacle? No. He said, 'It always seems impossible until it's done' and kept looking for new angles of attack. It's the same with all successful business people. It is not luck that keeps them at the top of their game; it's their tenacity to see setbacks as steps along the way to breakthroughs.

I am currently struggling to get my suppliers to upload their products to my online store. It's an unexpected setback for sure. When I asked myself how this could be fixed, breakthrough ideas started flowing. What if I could integrate their existing stores? Yes, that would remove me from being the support person, which is zapping a lot of my time. In a split second the thing that made me want to throw my business away sparked a new direction that had me energized and excited. I was already sending text messages to my web developer.

Don't be scared of changing your course or approach, but think twice about changing your dream to a smaller, more attainable one. What you're really giving up on is yourself.

Discoveries (formerly known as mistakes) and breakthroughs (formerly known as setbacks) are what this creative adventure is all about. It's one of the paradoxes of life: from the worst things come the best things.

Steve Jobs never set out to be fired from his own company, but if he hadn't, Pixar probably wouldn't exist. If he hadn't had his cancer scare, would he have been so driven to bring the iPhone and iPad into the world and live a life that excited him?

J. K. Rowling has famously said about the tricky situation she found herself in when she was forced to live below the poverty line after she with her new baby escaped from a violent relationship, "I was set free, because my greatest fear had already been realized, and I was still alive, and I still had a daughter whom I adored, and I had an old typewriter and a big idea. And so rock bottom became the solid foundation on which I rebuilt my life." If she had never found herself in such a mess, the Harry Potter books may have never touched the millions of lives that they have.

There are so many stories like this. Shit-storms have a way of blowing us in the right direction - if you let them.

REFLECTION

- How can your latest setback lead to a breakthrough?
- What are the opportunities in this obstacle?
- What alternative routes can I take to reach my goal?
- Name a time when an event or situation that seemed like the worst thing turned out to be a blessing in disguise.
- How can you remind yourself to embrace your obstacles in the future?
- How can you seek out obstacles in the future?

ACTION

- Get the poo out. The first attempt is going to be poo. It always is; it's cliche and unoriginal. But it's an important stepping-stone toward a great idea. When we expect the first attempt to be perfect, it can be impossible to start. By doing the opposite we set ourselves up for success. Set the intention to get the poo out, and move on to new ideas quickly.
- AFFIRM 'The first fifty sketches are going to be poo. They will really stink and that's what I want'.
- READ the autobiography of one of your heroes, and learn the struggles and determination it took to get them where they are today.

THE 'HOW' IS WHAT YOU GET

Cookies and cakes have the same ingredients, but it's the process that makes all the difference to the end result. If you stress and struggle to force your creative project, it will never hold the same positive energy as if you had fun with the process and enjoyed every moment of the journey.

Products of joy attract people who want to feel joy. But it isn't only happy people who can have a pleasant process. I am a big fan of dark art and sad songs because the cathartic, healing process of release that the artist felt when they made it translates into my own release when I experience it.

It's sayings like 'work hard' that trick us into thinking we need to work with a grimace on our face and a furrowed brow. All that body language does is tell your mind to create stress. Whether or not you think you need to struggle for creativity, either way you're right. So, invite yourself to have fun with it, and consider that what you feel when you create will determine the end result.

I wrote my master's thesis on a topic I was passionate about with the goal of making a difference. The pressure to change the world fell heavily on my shoulders, turning the thesis into a stressful experience. While I'm proud of what I achieved, I have no interest in publishing or promoting something that made me gain ten kilos and lose a handful of hair and a good chunk of my mind in the process. On the other hand, I love sharing the stories of how I created my artworks on holidays while backpacking overseas, and so do my customers. They want to take that happy energy and hang it up in their homes.

When you find yourself doing something a certain way, ask yourself why. Why do you think it needs to be done like this? Who taught you to do it that way? I found that I was approaching my design work too seriously, as if I were working a dead-end cubicle job out of the movie *Office Space*. Creative work is supposed to be fun. Add your flair to the process. Take your laptop to the beach, get a standing desk and dance as you work or make everything bright pink if that feels like you. Your creative process should be as unique as you are.

ACTION

Check in

Be aware of how you feel when you create, and check in with your body. If your body is tight, it will be a fight to get the creativity out of you. If you feel expansive and open, it will flow more freely. Try taking a pen to your mouth horizontally and biting on it for a minute or two. The forced smile will tell your mind it's happy. If you find yourself struggling, ask yourself how you want to feel. Create reminders around your space.

Channel the Feeling

Find an image that projects the vibe of the way you want to feel. I often work with a copy of the *Collective* magazine nearby, opened to a page with a young girl boss doing her thing. It reminds me to feel capable, rebellious and free.

Get in the Mood

Create a mood board in the theme of the feeling you want to invoke with magazines, on Pinterest or a mood board app. Keep it on display in your creative space.

Recommended Reading

If you're unsure of how you want to feel, Danielle Laporte's book *The Desire Map* is ground-breaking. Check it out! Her later book *How to be Loving* is also a must-read if you want to learn how to be kinder to yourself and at peace with the process.

TAKE A WALK ON THE WILD SIDE

When we are not limited by reality, society, technicalities, logic or even gravity we can really get creative. It is by suspending our perceptions and judgments that we open our minds to new ideas and solutions. Sure, they may not work in the current reality, but can we change reality? Anything is possible.

How would you feel if I asked you to give me your wildest idea? You might feel a little silly, childish and even like you're wasting time. For many it doesn't feel comfortable or natural. But 'wild' by definition is to be in a natural state. We were born with wild brains that have the power to imagine anything, the power to come up with the most innovative solutions ever invented. So, what happened?

School happened. Schools use grading systems for marking efficiency. Rather than finding as many ideas as possible, creative ideas or even the best idea, schools teach that the only idea that matters is the correct one. There is only one correct answer, and everything else is wrong. So, we disown that magical part of our brains and become tame (and lame).

Your wild innovation centre may have lain dormant for years, even decades, but it never goes away. You can be a remedial creative genius by embracing who you were born to be and inviting it back.

After years of scolding for being 'wrong', it may take some coaxing to feel safe. Assure yourself that those critical teachers are long gone by harnessing the power of play. It's difficult to be afraid when you are being playful. Play takes you back to a time in your life before you had that inner critic telling you what is right and wrong. Play invites mistakes. Play's only rule is to have fun.

ACTION

Create a 'play' toolkit: My secret weapons for initiating play are colourful markers, crayons, butcher's paper, Post-it notes and fun music. I recommend taking a stroll down the kid's stationary section of your supermarket to create your own toolkit for play. Give your inner child some cash to buy whatever he or she or they want.

Use your non-dominant hand to come up with ideas or sketches. This will throw perfectionism right out the window!

Talk to your inner child: Write a question to your younger self. Then using a different coloured marker, use your non-dominant hand to write the response. You may be surprised with what comes out. Keep the conversation going!

Write or draw with your eyes closed: There's no better way to silence your inner critic than to hide what you're creating.

Speed drawing: Come up with as many ideas as fast as you can. Draw thirty circles on a sheet of paper or google '30 Circles Challenge' to print a worksheet. In sixty seconds turn each circle into something different.

The 'what if' game: What if the walls were made of cheese? What if we could breathe underwater? What if we could only communicate with touch? Ask yourself a series of such questions to prime your brain to think differently.

Role play: Put yourself in the shoes of someone completely different: Picasso, the head of Apple, or an alien from another planet. Anyone!

Dress ups: Maybe you can have a pair of glasses or a thinking hat that you can use when you play. Maybe by dressing up you can take your role-play persona to another level!

A letter from the future: Sometimes when we can't see the solution, it can help to imagine as if it were already solved. Write yourself a letter from your future self or a wise future leader telling you what to do.

3
MAKE UP

Creative living is hard work balanced with a softness toward the self. Are you ready to surrender?

SELF-COMPASSION

Practicing your craft, studying the masters, analysing the success of others and learning how to network and promote yourself are important (and anxiety-provoking) parts of being the best creative person that you can be. But before you can succeed at any of them fully, you need to learn the most underrated skill ever: being kind to yourself.

Becoming Failure Friendly will force you to be honest with yourself about the reasons for your creative blocks and anxiety. Spoiler alert: when you get to the bottom of it, the reason is *you*. Realising that the only thing holding you back is you—or, rather, your subconscious thoughts—does not usually provoke self-compassion.

My first reaction was anger. I mentally berated myself with thoughts like, 'You're so pathetic. You've done this to yourself. What hope do you have? You're a horrible person." As cruel and twisted as it may seem, you can't fight hate with hate or fear with fear. Just as only light can end darkness, only love and self-compassion can end the cycle of self-hate and the fearful thinking patterns telling you that you're not good enough.

You may have been brought up by well-meaning parents who wanted only for you to grow into an outstanding citizen. Your parents may have done their best to teach you many life lessons, which may have sounded like, 'Why did you kick the ball in the house when I've told you not to? Do you see how stupid that was? You should have known better! That window is going to be very expensive to fix, you know! You can go to bed early for being so careless'.

We often grow up learning that if we do something bad, we are bad and deserve a scolding or punishment, to teach us not to be bad again. When we step into the real world, in an effort to be responsible, we try to parent ourselves with harsh words. 'You're such an idiot for leaving this to the last minute', when what we really mean is, 'Next time let's get onto this project early to avoid the stress of missing deadlines'.

Piling on put-downs in an effort to teach yourself a lesson for the future is counterproductive. It may feel responsible to be harsh with yourself, but it is not helpful. Let go of your need to belittle yourself after a mistake and instead turn to loving yourself, forgiving yourself, not taking things so seriously, having some perspective, showing self-compassion, being kind to yourself, whatever you want to call it.

This gentle skill is the key to living a long and prosperous creative life. Like any new skill though, it takes practice to develop.

ACTION

In your creative space, place a small mirror and a photograph of you as a child (preferably showing your hands and smiling). Whenever you feel the need to criticise yourself, look at that photo and then into your eyes before asking yourself if you would say those things to this innocent child. Just as it's inappropriate to crush a child's spirit, it's inappropriate to do it to your adult self. Look into your eyes in the mirror and tell yourself kindly what you need to say. Words such as 'I love and approve of you', 'I accept you', 'I believe in you', 'I have your back' and 'You can do this' are among some of the most powerful things you can say when feeling hopelessly stuck.

MEDITATION

The next time you feel your body flood with anxiety, anger or any other uncomfortable feeling, try this self-compassion meditation.

1. FEEL IT TO HEAL IT: Check in with yourself, and do a body scan from head to toe to identify where in your body you feel this uncomfortable sensation. What does it feel like?

2. NAME IT TO TAME IT: Now that you feel it, can you name the feeling—not the story or reason for it but merely the name of the emotion? Finish this sentence 'I feel (insert emotions here)'. If you're still learning emotional literacy, naming the physical sensation is a great way to start.

3. SOFTEN AND SOOTHE: Without judgement, sit with that emotion or sensation for a moment and let your breath and self-compassion soften the edges of it. Place your hand on your chest and rub your heart clockwise to help ease and release it. You don't need a pep talk; you just need a moment to feel it.

You can also listen to a guided self-compassion meditation here: http://self-compassion.org/category/exercises/

DETACHMENT

Is something blocking you from diving headfirst into your creativity? This section is about letting go of the baggage and the beliefs that are standing in your way.

WARNING: Keep an open mind as you read this next section. I am not asking you to accept these theories as true because I honestly don't know if they are. But what I know for sure is that if you allow yourself to try on these beliefs, your life will work better. Things like success and creativity become easier. Maybe it's a lie you have to tell yourself to create. But if the woo-woo sets you free, and it's not hurting anyone, who cares?

OTHER PEOPLE

For many of my childhood years, I was woken early by the sound of my brother playing his guitar. Every night I would bang on the wall, unable to fall asleep to the sound of his strumming. Every. Single. Day. And it wasn't that songs that he can play now. No, it was musical scales and stopping and starting because he had made a mistake. It was the music of madness. Today he is a talented musician who seems at one with his instrument. Just like all successful creatives, no one remembers those years of mistakes or the music of madness that led to his success.

With the struggle out of sight, many of us can look to people ahead of us and feel that if we do have to work hard for it, we are failing in some way, or perhaps it's a sign we don't deserve it. Creative people are particularly vulnerable to the destructive nature of comparison, judging our insides by other people's outsides.

When I was in my early twenties, I would spend hours stalking the Facebook accounts of friends, acquaintances and even acquaintances of friends, the people who were travelling the world and seemed to have it all together. It would send me into a rut of despair about the state of my life. At the same time, the people who were pregnant and were living a life of responsibility made me feel a little better about my endless freedom. Temporarily.

Comparison erodes our self-worth even when we use it to look down on people. It's a temporary high that feeds a lie, the lie that what's on the outside counts more than what's on the inside.

I didn't realise how much I cared about my own veneer until I recently felt the shame of admitting there were cracks. It was something I had never heard anyone talk about, so I assumed I must be the only one, that there was something wrong with me. I held it in for nearly a year until it was so bad that I couldn't ignore it. What I was scared to admit was that I experienced pain during sex. By not dealing with it, I had conditioned by body to associate sex with pain, leaving my muscles sore from the constant tensing. When asked why I had stopped exercising, I came clean. To my bewilderment the first three women I told had had similar experiences and knew exactly what I was going through. The relief!

When we open up about our human emotions, it triggers activity in the frontal lobe of the brain, diverting blood flow from fight-or-flight centers and reducing stress. Additionally, feeling heard and respected during this process releases estrogen and bonding chemicals that give us a positive emotional boost. Moreover, exploring our emotions often leads us to identify solutions and answers within ourselves.

So, talk about it! Talk about your struggles, and know that if you're experiencing it, other people are too. You're not that special that it only happens to you, sorry!

By sharing our creative struggles, we give all creatives permission to accept their process and persevere through the difficulties. It's also your job to listen to the struggles of those around you. Never shame anyone else for standing bare. You don't need to solve it for them either, simply stand beside them.

Learning to love our struggles and processes is essential to becoming who we are meant to be. It's like the girl who tried to help the butterfly break out of its cocoon - by removing the struggle, the butterfly emerged weaker and unable to fly. Our struggles and processes are what make us strong and help us become the best version of ourselves.

REFLECTION

Look for the lessons in your current creative struggle. What is it teaching you? How is it making you stronger? List all the reasons why you love your struggle.

THE EGO

If you're a writer who is told by a publisher your writing isn't good enough, then it is easy to conclude that you are not good enough. But it's not true. (This is what happens when we forget to frame things with a growth mindset. What would have been more accurate would be to say 'Your writing is not good enough *yet*'.)

Attaching your self-worth to your work, your accomplishments, your body or your possessions is the trap of the ego. The ego is a false idea of who you are that compares you to others and places meaning only on the external. It tells you that you are separate from others and that the opinions of others are more important than your own.

The yogi Osho said that, 'The ego is the greatest disease that can happen to man. A big ego is like a rock blocking your path. While a small ego results in an inferiority complex, making you afraid to try or expect failure which of course ensures failure'.

Do you identify as creative, a writer, an actor, a painter, a musician or an artist first and a human second? If you've tied the success of your creative endeavours to your personal worth it's no wonder you're having a hard time making a move. The stakes are too high!

If I was to tell you that you need to let the whole '(insert your creative field here)' thing go, that it's not who you really are, how would you feel? For me it was like having my skin ripped off.

When the opportunity to do a workshop with one of my street art idols came up, I jumped at the chance. I brought my boyfriend at the time along who was not a particularly arty person but liked trying new things. My experience at the workshop was not what I expected.

All of my ideas for the group mural were changed, and my artistic ability was not taken seriously. I was left making a piece of 'filler' art to merely join other peoples' 'real' art pieces (or so my ego told me). I tried to focus on how much I was learning instead of my disappointment in making a piece of art I wouldn't put my name to, but it was obvious I wasn't enjoying myself.

My not-so-arty boyfriend, who now was creating a beautiful tree design next to my stupid 'swoosh', asked me what was wrong. I said it was nothing, but he dug and dug, asking why it hurt me so much to have my ideas changed. I eventually screamed, 'Art is my 'thing'! It's who I am!'

He had the gall to say, 'Why don't you just let go of the idea you're an artist?'

'What?' I replied. 'Then I'm nothing!' I stormed off and went home—and this is where it gets embarrassing. I was crying violently with a pile of my painted canvases in front of me as I took a knife and stabbed them with all my might. Like a full-blown crazy person, I stabbed and stabbed as I wailed.

It was sad to destroy work that seemed like a part of me, but the destruction felt good. I think I might have yelled 'Die! as I stabbed. Every single canvas was covered in stab wounds. The force of the blows even rubbed skin off my hand.

When all the tears were cried and all of the art was 'dead', there was peace. A weight was lifted. The art was dead, and I was still alive. I had released the artist identity I had clung to, and I was okay without it.

It's the same sort of clarity you get when you see a loved one's body after they pass away. Their body and everything they ever worked for remains, but they are gone. Their 'spirit' has left the building, and everything that remains is meaningless without it.

If I took away your house, your things, your talents, your achievements, your looks, all the things that you believe make you special, you would still be something. And no matter what you do or don't do, it never changes. It's always perfect. It's life force. It's energy. And it's real.

The suggestion to let go of everything I thought I was (an artist) was my invitation to connect with my true self. A more peaceful way to do this is to acknowledge that the ego can only exist through tension. It cannot reign supreme when you are truly relaxed.

Buddha said, 'Be driftwood, float with the stream and let it take you to the ocean'. This is not permission to be lazy; it is guidance to be peaceful as you take action toward your creative goals instead of forcing your way through life.

Embrace the success or failure of others as our own. Celebrate them equally to dismantle the illusion of separation and competition between us. If they can do it, it's proof that you can too!

REFLECTION

How can you build a relaxation practice into your creative process?

ACTION

Give it away: To detach from the externally constructed idea of who you are, give away your possessions, especially the ones you feel most attached to, and enjoy the lightness.

Shout out: Once a week share one of your peers' work or success. Celebrate them!

MASCULINITY

I'm a female who struggles with femininity. I have always felt that to be girly is to be weak. I refuse to dress like a girl, to listen to music like a girl, to play sports like a girl (playing netball would be such a sin, a sport where you wear a skirt—no thanks). I refuse to engage in the girly dialogue of 'I'm so fat', 'No you're not, I'm way fatter', 'But look at this muffin top, I'm disgusting' (I still don't understand the point of this frustrating game that girls play). It all just seemed so...inferior.

I thought I did a good job of steering away from the insanity of girly-ness. I was able to see through the marketing that targeted women's insecurities. Shaving, waxing, plucking, makeup, cover up, contouring, fake tan, fake lashes, hair straightening, hair curling, hair dying, hair styling, perfume, nail polish, detoxing, dieting, push-up bras, slimming, sculpting, age defying, skin perfecting, teeth whitening, retouching—all exhausting activities to hide who we really are, created for the sole purpose of making men rich. I wanted no part of it.

It wasn't until watching the powerful documentary *The Mask We Wear,* which illuminates the many ways boys are relentlessly told that in order to 'be a man' they must reject femininity that it hit me. The link this has on the dehumanisation of women and the violence against them shook me to my core.

Whether it's in sports, movies, music, business or politics, the idolisation of males, or females who behave like males, who are always in control of their emotions, always charging and ready to deal with conflict by inflicting it on others through revenge or one-upping, is destroying our society.

I didn't even understand what femininity was, besides the ability to cry, until I watched the documentary. As I watched, it became clear that femininity isn't weakness; it's strength.

My default approach to life's challenges is to charge into them, force my way through, and make it happen. When I pump myself up for a creative challenge, I begin to motivate myself by laying on the pressure. 'This is important. People are watching. Do you want to look like an idiot, or do you want to prove yourself?' A toxic masculine and aggressive approach seemed the best one.

When things get hard, I'd take the motivation up a notch, and pressure turns to shame. I tell myself, 'You're a failure. You're a piece of . . .' It's the tough love that I think I need to succeed.

I have another side that comes out when there is no pressure, usually when I have given up and surrendered. This side is softer, gracious and forgiving. In this state I have the ability to let go of the anger I've been holding onto tightly, like a hot coal burning my hand.

This softer side can release pain and create peace. This is real femininity.

If you are a man or a woman who sees femininity as a weakness and prefers to aggressively push through life, I have a truth bomb for you: **Femininity is freedom from the fear of being weak. Femininity is knowing that you are strong. When you're in your feminine power, nothing can hurt you because pain is the source of healing. It's the warrior so strong that she doesn't need to fight**.

The more I explore divine femininity, the more answers I find. Feminine energy, like creative energy, is cyclical—periodic times of intense focus and flow followed by long periods of rest. Learning to listen to your body and allowing it to rest is crucial if you want to sustain a highly creative lifestyle.

Feminine energy, like creativity energy, is magnetic. It doesn't need to charge and force; it is an open vessel for inspiration. I'm still learning how to be more receptive. When I am at my best, ideas always come, and creative work becomes a pleasure.

All emotions serve a purpose. So, the next time you are facing a crisis of confidence, I urge you to embrace your feminine power, let your walls down and be that safe womb of support for yourself as you express whatever is bubbling inside.

REFLECTION

- What does it mean to be a man? Why? Why? Why? Why? Why?

- What does it mean to be a female? Why? Why? Why? Why? Why?

- What is masculinity?

- What is femininity?

- What does femininity mean to you? Why? Why? Why? Why? Why?

- What is stopping you from embracing your femininity? Why?

- When was the last time you embraced your feminine power? What did it feel like?

- Can you think of a time when you surrendered to your pain? What happened?

- If you were not afraid of feeling pain, how would that affect your creative life?

- How can you own your femininity?

HIGHER POWER

When I say, 'higher power', I do not mean a force that dictates your life or nullifies your power. You are your own higher power. It's the untapped energy that we all have access to but rarely harness.

Words like 'higher power', 'God' or 'spirituality' are easy to scoff at when you want to be in control of your life and your creativity. I was very closed off to anything spiritual because religion was the source of all evil in my eyes (from genocides to child abuse, discrimination and endless suffering it all seemed to be justified by 'God'). And besides, the science just didn't add up (A virgin mother? Please!). But then I discovered quantum physics.

Quantum physics strangely aligns with many traditional spiritual teachings from Australian Aboriginal principles to Native Hawaiian philosophy and even the ancient teachings of yoga. These wisdom traditions focus on everything in existence being interconnected or 'one'. Quantum physics, which is all about energy, proves that all things that are made up of atoms are, in fact, made up of pure energy. The same 'one', energy if you will.

When I learned that science mirrors spiritual wisdom, I started to pay attention. I learned that this energy we are all made up of is constantly vibrating at different frequencies. 'Good vibes' and 'bad vibes' were no longer woo-woo but scientific—positive energy vibrations and negative energy vibrations. Not only are we made up of energy, we all came from the same energy source and are all still invisibly linked. If this is new to you, it will sound far out, but do some research, (Michio Kaku the scientist behind String Field Theory is a good place to start), and you'll find that this is solid stuff.

If we are all, in fact, vibrating energy, by changing our thoughts we can alter the vibrational frequency around us to change our current reality. It sounds crazy, but even Einstein proclaimed that, 'Everything is energy, and that's all there is to it. Match the frequency of the reality you want, and you cannot help but get that reality. It can be no other way. This is not philosophy. This is physics'. The Law of Attraction (explored in the movie *The Secret*) is actually the Law of Physics.

The power of mind over matter has been beautifully demonstrated by Japanese scientist Dr. Masaru Emoto, who performed a series of experiments observing the physical effect of words and prayers on water. His photographs showed that when water was exposed to positive, loving thoughts or prayer, the transformation was remarkable. Negative words left the frozen water 'blobby' while positive blessing transformed the frozen water so that, under a microscope, it appeared as delicate snowflake designs, similar to jewels. This change occurred purely from having positive words taped to the container or positive thoughts directed at it. No joke! When humans are made up of 70 percent water it's not hard to imagine how positive words, thoughts and beliefs can change us on a cellular level too.

So, while I can't buy into the idea of a man with a white beard passing judgment from the clouds, I can make peace with there being an invisible energy field around us that we are made of, that due to our limited senses we cannot fully perceive or comprehend. That it links all things, making all things and events interconnected. That because of this one energy we can affect and change our reality through thoughts and prayer. Some people call this energy 'God' or 'the Universe' or simply 'Love'. I call it the power of the mind because, as an ex-atheist, that works for me.

> **REFLECTION**
>
> Do you believe in a higher power? Why or why not?
>
> How would believing in a higher power and its ability to support you change the way you approach your creative projects?

DIVINE INSPIRATION

For creative people who are often labeled 'artistic' or 'talented', it can be too easy to buy into your ego and feel the pressure of living up to your own label. I mentioned the story earlier of my first art studio where I tormented myself with the impossible goal of proving my talent. The pressure and fear of failure can be devastating for our productivity and mental health, which is why I love the theory that Elizabeth Gilbert puts forth in her book *Big Magic*.

Gilbert recommends creatives choose to embrace the idea that creativity comes from a higher source that uses us as a vessel. She suggests that we *have* a genius or a divine power that flows through us, rather than us *being* a genius. Whether this theory rings true for you or not, you have to admit it's nice to take the pressure off.

When you think about that moment of inspiration, can you articulate where it comes from? It's mysterious and powerful. When you're inspired, suddenly all of your cells come alive, you have more energy and focus than normal and you don't need to sleep or eat; it just flows. Ancient societies believed that inspiration was actually the call of God or the gods, that being inspired was being in a higher state of consciousness as the divine energy flowed through them.

The origin of the word 'inspiration' translated to being 'in spirit'. When we are inspired, we live 'in spirit' with a greater purpose and less attachment to the physical or the unreal. What if your creative work was a spiritual act?

Michelangelo described the divinity of inspiration best when he said, 'I saw the angel in the marble and carved until I set him free'. Seeing inspiration and creativity in this way makes it much easier to release the ego and the pressure. **By embracing a higher power that flows through you but is not of you, you are off the hook.**

You may have gathered by now that I am a fan of yoga. In yoga the greeting 'Namaste' means 'the divinity in me recognises the divinity in you. When we are both in that space, we are one.' This sums up the ideas in this section of the book. Divine creative energy is always available for us to tap into if we let go of expectations, competition and what other people think.

When we turn up as willing and humble vessels, creativity will flow through us, connecting us to everything else. But it's important to remember it is not of us.

REFLECTION & ACTION

When I notice worries appear regarding what other people think of me or how I compare, I like to affirm the following: 'Creativity comes through me, but it is not of me'. Is there an affirmation or a reminder to stop interfering with the process that works for you? Display it in your creative space, and make it the prayer used to call on the Saint of Creativity.

SACRED RITUALS

Carving out time for anything that fills you up (getting inspired, reading, meditating, nature, fun, exercise or friends) is critically important for your creative journey. Filling up the tank equips you to face those long and winding roads.

Life hackers advise us to harness the power of habits to establish non-negotiable wellness practices. If you want to fast-track and habitualise a new practice, start doing that activity in unison with an existing habit, something you currently do without thinking about, e.g. brushing your teeth or relieving your bladder in the morning. I have used this trick to establish my morning ritual: RPM (rise, pee, meditate, inspired by Davidji).

But like everything, there are two ways of looking at habits: through the eyes of fear or love.

Fear	Love
Habits	Rituals
Sacrifices	Sacred Practices
Rationale: "I need to create a habit of sacrificing twenty minutes of my busy day to just sit there and do nothing."	Rationale: "I want to create a sacred ritual for myself to connect to stillness for twenty minutes a day"

While I admit habits are powerful, as a creative thinker, I am naturally rebellious. I rebel against anything that seems repetitive unless it is sacred to me. By making a practice sacred, it becomes a symbolic act with an honouring focus to feed the spirit. It becomes about connecting with a higher power.

One of my sacred rituals is the way I order my to-do list. I have one column for the 'to do's' and one for the unplanned 'dones' that spring up on me. I colour code the completed items with a highlighter, then at the end of the day I use a different colour to highlight the undone tasks to carry on to the next day. I've continued to do it this way even though I'm naturally a bit sloppy and chaotic. I've learned to enjoy keeping it clean and organised because it makes a huge difference to how I feel about my work. If it feels special to you, it is sacred.

Sacred rituals are not just great for establishing desired habits but signifying that you are about to start creating. A ritual or ceremony can prime your mind to get you into a flow state of channelling creativity. One of the frustrations for many creative people is that they cannot turn their creativity on or off then they want to. Ceremonies can help with this. Light a candle, say a prayer, take a deep breath or go for a walk. Find a practice that suits you. Make it special, and keep it sacred.

TIP

What is a habit or ritual you do every day without fail? Can you add a secondary habit to this practice?

For example, if you brush your teeth at the same time every day, can you journal for ten minutes straight after that? Place your journal with your toothbrush, and try it for twenty-one days (the number of days that research suggests is needed to form a new habit).

Wait until one habit is well established before adding a new one.

If you are rebellious, it may be a good idea to mix up your ritual. For example, maybe it's not the same time every day, or if it is, it's not the exact same practice. Spice it up when you can!

ACTION

Create two sacred rituals to signify the start and end of your creative process. Be consistent with them. After a while your creativity will know when it's time to show up. I have found that no matter how much I would love my creative juices to flow from nine to five, it just doesn't work that way. Such high energy cannot be sustained for eight hours a day, so be kind to yourself until you find what works for you.

Sometimes sacred rituals require sacred items like a special stationary or a lucky accessory. Find something that you feel holds positive energy, and incorporate it into your ritual. Second hand stores and are great places for finding creative props that have story and character, no need to break the bank for your creativity.

GO!

Feel fear and do it anyway.

FAILURE FRIENDLY

BUZZY LEWIS

FEEL FEAR AND DO IT ANYWAY

If you, like me, went through your entire creative education without the mention of mental preparation, except for the blatant remark 'You have to deal with criticism if you want to be a designer', you probably are not equipped with strategies to deal with the anxiety that arises on the creative journey. You do your best, fluking results and sometimes falling into dark holes. Before I set out on my journey to 'figure it out', I had three strategies for dealing with creative anxiety.

1. **Freeze:** I would wait for inspiration, which rarely came. The longer I waited, the harder it was to start, until I couldn't start. The pressure that I would choke was too great. This didn't serve me.

2. **Flight:** I would eject myself from the stressful situation by resisting the anxiety under the guise of procrastination. YouTube videos, social media and food were where I could be found when a creative deadline was looming. While it made me feel better temporarily, it didn't serve me either.

3. **Fight:** After wasting the time on the first two responses, my inner critic would kick in and want to see results. I would become my own worst enemy. 'You idiot! Why have you wasted so much time? Get moving!' This unpleasant strategy served me the least and more often than not made me revert back to freezing.

Sometimes it seemed the only thing that actually got me started was admitting defeat (releasing the ego).

I became a creative because I loved the exhilaration of using my mind to come up with ideas. But it seemed that the same mind was working against me. I had talent, passion, skills and a university degree, but it didn't count for anything if I couldn't do the one thing that I wanted to do: create!

If this sounds like you, hear this: if I can get to the other side, so can you. I will take you through my strategies for getting out of freeze, flight and fight for those times when you find yourself stuck. I'm also happy to say that you have other options. In this chapter I will share my secret strategies for meeting fear first as a **friend** and then as a **leader**.

FREEZE & FLIGHT – BREAKING THE PATTERN

When you are drowning in a sea of your own thoughts, you need to break the thought pattern and get out of your head. As much as we can analyse our thoughts and beg ourselves to think differently, when you are truly stuck, the best way is not to think or feel but act. By changing your behaviour, you will change your thoughts. Forget about the project's pressure for a moment and try the following.

ACTION

Breath: Take a big, deep breath, slowly through your nose, filling your lungs and stomach, and then slowly release it. The surge of oxygen is what your body needs. Take a few minutes to breathe deeply. When we're stressed, we forget to breathe. When our breathing is shallow, our brains think something is wrong and produce adrenaline, which leads to more stress. The simplest thing you can do is breathe.

Pause: A breathing technique that can distract you from the monkey mind is to breathe deeply and focus your attention on the pause between the exhale and inhale. Try to hold it for a little longer each time, for as long as it's comfortable. As this gap of stillness grows, it leaves less room for crazy thoughts. You can also do this by blocking one nostril to inhale through your left, hold, then exhale through your right nostril and so on. This technique has been used in yoga for centuries to calm and cleanse the body and balance the left and right brain as well as our masculine and feminine energy.

Keep Your Head Up: Sit or stand up straight, hold your shoulders back, lift your chin and puff out your chest. This will not only make it easier to breathe deeply, it is also your body's way of telling your mind you feel confident and powerful. Research shows that holding a power stance for two minutes can greatly increase your confidence.

Tap That: EFT (Emotional Freedom Technique) tapping is a simple technique that is actually quite difficult to explain. I recommend watching a YouTube video to learn how it works. Start by rating your current level of anxiety out of ten. Then state it to yourself: 'Even though I have this 9/10 anxiety that makes me feel scared, I completely love and accept myself'. As you continue to describe how you feel, tap your fingers on certain trigger points on your body in a certain order, mostly around your face. The repetitive tapping calms the racing amygdala in your brain. By the end of the sequence, tell yourself you've calmed down and then re-rate and state your anxiety level. You will find it does work.

Power Nap: A short nap of twenty to thirty minutes can help to improve mood, alertness and performance. It has been proven to have lasting effects to reduce stress in the body. Just the act of lying horizontal for twenty minutes has been proven to be beneficial for stress levels. Nappers are in good company. Winston Churchill, John F. Kennedy, Ronald Reagan, Napoleon, Albert Einstein, Thomas Edison and George W. Bush are all known to have valued an afternoon nap.

Mediate: In its simplest form, meditation is sitting and concentrating on your breath instead of your monkey mind thoughts, which jump from one thing to the next without rest. The trick to stillness is using an anchor (breathing, mantras, body awareness, present moment awareness, the senses or visualisations). For greater stillness I recommend listening to a guided meditation on SoundCloud or YouTube. My personal favorite is Davidji on SoundCloud because it takes me back to meditating in India with chanting, mantras or mudras.

Moving Meditation: Purge your fear thoughts through walking, running, swimming, surfing, yoga, team sports or whatever feels fun for you. Dancing and singing in your office can be a great way to shake off fears!

Journaling: To stop your thoughts from swimming uncontrollably around your head, it can help to write them down or even illustrate them. Get them out of your head and onto paper and then leave them there.

BE CURIOUS

Your fearful thoughts are like ghosts. When you freeze in front of them, you lose your power. When you run from them, you give them even more power over you. Running promises relief but delivers only worry. When you run you become their prisoner, haunted by their taunts. But ghosts only exist in darkness. If you have the courage to face them in the light, they will disappear.

You're nearly ready to approach your fear. Before you can fight your enemy though, you need to study your enemy's moves.

Resistance comes in many forms. It may be eating too much, cleaning when you should be working or playing video games instead of starting that project. Eating, cleaning and entertainment on their own are all important parts of life. It's not the activity that's the issue; it's the intention. Eating for nourishment is fine. Eating to fill an empty hole in your life is not. Have you ever caught yourself mindlessly eating, suddenly to realize what you're shovelling into your mouth doesn't actually taste very good and that you're not even hungry? That aha moment of mindfulness is what we are after. Before you can address your resistance, you need to become aware of it.

ACTION

It's time to become a detective. Learn to turn off your judgment, and turn up your curiosity. Watching yourself from a distance, try to answer these questions:

What are the triggers that set off your resistance?

What do you do when you're triggered?

How does that make you feel?

What are you saying to yourself throughout the experience?

Can you see any interesting patterns?

Stay curious as you begin to delve a little deeper.

Reappraise the situation. Is it really as dangerous as you think?

Is there a similar situation in the past that you have overcome?

Is your self-talk something you would say to a friend?

What do you think the fear is trying to tell you?

Stay curious for as long as you need to. The more information you have on the inner workings of your fears, the easier it will be to predict their movements when you approach during the next step. Remember, you can always come back to this step to regain clarity.

'A JOURNEY OF A THOUSAND MILES STARTS WITH ONE SINGLE STEP' ~LAO TZU

The first step toward facing your fear can be the hardest because the ego screams the loudest right before you do. In its last chance to retain control, it creates an uncomfortable energy in your body, an erratic, constricted vibration like butterflies in your tummy. I call it feeling 'my fire'. It can be so unbearable that you want to run. It is the same energy you feel when you ride a roller-coaster, when you buy flights for your dream holiday, or when you answer the door to your hot date. In those situations you call it excitement. There is a fine line between fear and excitement. Physiologically, they're identical. You have the power to decide what your 'fire' means. Is it unbearable dread or an exciting opportunity?

Think of the last time you were truly excited. What did you do? Did you jump for joy? Throw your hands in the air? Smile? The fire you feel is your body producing the chemicals for fight or flight, readying you for action. While I have recommended taking a moment to break the pattern while you feel frozen, when you feel the fire, it's time to get that energy out. It wants to move. Jump and jive or punch a pillow or the sky if that feels good. Do what you do when you're truly excited to tell your mind you got this.

When you are excited about something you don't need to motivate yourself to do it because you can't wait to get started. Doing your version of a happy dance is taking fear and using it to fuel your fire. Speaking of fire, this is a note I keep next to my to-do list:

Let's get this fire started.
Like the best firewood, you need to break it down,
way down, kindling, baby!
The smaller the better!
Don't smother your flame with a heavy load.
Lighten up and watch it light up!
Excitement is the spark.

Just like a fire, you need to start your creative process with small steps. Not because you're stepping into the unknown but because that's the only way you can get anything done. Big steps like publishing a book or launching your website may seem impressive, but in reality, they are just the sum of many small steps that you have taken. The final step can be the easiest because of the momentum you have built up behind you.

Say you've got a goal to write a book. What is the smallest step you can take toward it? Most people say, 'Write a few pages a day'. That is not small. That is like trying to set a log on fire. When I say, 'small', I mean tinier than tiny. Seemingly insignificant steps are what you need to start with. Whatever you think of as your first step, cut it in half, make it smaller again and then think of ten steps before that.

Start with writing down the first three tiny steps. Step one needs to be something like: 'Step into the studio, sit at the desk and turn on the computer'. These things alone can be scary when you know where they lead. Do not underestimate their importance.

By giving yourself easy wins like 'brush teeth', you immediately start ticking things off your list. Feeling the momentum is all you need to get on a roll. You also get a release of dopamine every time you tick something off, which will make you crave more. If you do a task that was not originally on the list, write it down, so you can tick it off too, giving you the dopamine you deserve. If you feel your momentum slowing, access your action steps. Have you underestimated their size? Do they need to be broken down further?

WARNING: If during this process you hear your inner critic saying, 'You pathetic baby, taking your baby steps', remember this is the voice of fear. Remind it that, 'Small steps are all there is. Big steps are an illusion', or just 'Thanks for sharing, but I got this'.

ACTION

The 5 WHYS is a great way to get to the core of the fear, to find out what is really going on in your subconscious. Don't be scared as you delve deep to find out what your mind is really telling you. Every answer your mind gives you, ask it again and again Why or 'Y'. Do this at least five times to get to the root of what is going on. Then force yourself to flip the fear on its head and generate reasons why it's also exciting. You'll be pleasantly surprised by the positive reasons your magnet mind will produce. Close the practice with gratitude for what you have discovered and how you can use this information moving forward. This gratitude statement is what you can return to when the fearful voices butt into your creative process.

FACE IT: I feel anxious about . . . *(e.g., Starting because it's new)*

Y	
Y	
Y	
Y	
Y	

FLIP IT: I am excited about . . . *(e.g., Starting because I'm ready to learn)*

Y	
Y	
Y	
Y	
Y	

FREE IT: SAY CHEERS FEARS!!!

I am grateful for this fear because it is telling me that . . .

So I can . . .

CHECK YOUR CHECKLISTS

It's helpful to start at your end goal and then work backwards to plan all the steps you need to take, but this is not a checklist; this is a plan. Having a list like this with a full page of action steps in front of you while you work can set you up to fail. It can make you feel heavy and overwhelmed. As you tick things off, your momentum will feel painfully slow against your one-, three- or six-month plan. Make this your master list. Only review it at the start or the end of the week when you set your smaller weekly goals.

In line with your weekly goals, your daily list should have no more than three items on it. Anything more scatters your focus. It's fine to do more, but add them to the list after the first three are complete. This underrated tip has been key to me getting things done. Another approach that works is to use a Post-it note to cover items two and three while you work on one and then move it down as you progress. By focusing on one thing at a time, you will keep fear and distractions at bay while getting more done. Another quirky tip I learned from Les Watson the 'Time Lord' and productivity coach at Get More Time in Geelong, is that instead of ticking or crossing out the completed items, highlight them. There is something about colour blocking that communicates the progress in a powerful way. Become a monotasker!

If you've had the same action step on your to-do list for one week or more, it's too big. You need to break it down to make it achievable. Support yourself with tasks you can do easily rather than taunting yourself with the recurring reminder of your failure. 'But I should be able to do it; it's tiny', you may find yourself saying. Maybe it's a phone call or an email you need to send that will literally take five minutes. In this case there is a step you need to take first: overcoming the resistance you are clearly facing. Yes, if small items don't get ticked off after a few days, you are resisting them. Get your detective hat and your journal out, and ask your resistance why, why, why, why, why? Ask it what it needs. Perhaps a draft script for the call, practicing what you need to say or doing some research is all it needs. Maybe you just need a reality check. Tell your resistance you are not under attack and that you will not die if the call isn't perfect. It's all part of the process.

WARNING: This is a phase of getting to know what's attainable and what's too ambitious. You won't get it perfect the first time, and it will take time to find what size steps work for you. The first few weeks are about tracking or auditing what you can and can't do. Be kind to yourself as you refine it along the way. It's an experiment.

The Failure Friendly Mindset is all about growth and tipping the scales away from fear and towards faith. With this in mind, it can be fun to create a reverse to-do list or a value list. I started this ritual when I wanted to make more money. As money is just a substitute for value, I needed to create more value and realize my current value. As I did things that created value, from exercising to networking to researching, I would write them down to become aware of them. Throughout the day the list would grow and grow, reminding me of how far I had come in a short time. If you find yourself feeling behind and having a pity party, you need to turn it into a 'progress party'. It's as simple as shifting your focus to how far you've come rather than how much farther you have to go, make a list of your accomplishments. Seeing your progress in this way can be like rocket fuel to get you going again.

The paradoxes at work here are that 'small steps make a big difference' and 'by doing less you do more'. While I champion small steps and small lists, I chase big ideas. When I worked a demanding job at a busy beauty company, my daily activity list grew longer each day. This was where I learned to 'fake it till you make it'. Every morning when I looked at the list and the deadlines next to each item—'one hour to create an advertisement for Vogue', 'two hours to create a monthly newsletter'—the logical side of my brain knew it was literally impossible. But that year my manta was 'too easy'. Even though it felt like a lie, I'd look at the list and say, 'Yep, too easy', and somehow, I always get it done, one thing at a time. Don't underestimate small steps, the power of focus, or yourself.

A SIDE NOTE ON FOCUS: Don't fall into the trap of dealing with emails or messages as they come in. These little distractions take you fifteen to forty-five minutes to refocus on what you were meant to be doing. Batch it! Set times in the day when you will read and respond, and possibly set up an automatic email response alerting people to your 'allocated creative studio time' so they know to call you if urgent. You won't believe how much time this saves.

FIGHT – WHAT DID YOU JUST SAY?

You need to make a move on this creative project because time is slipping away. You're sick of wasting hours and feeling helpless. It's crunch time. You'll take matters into your own hands. You tell the fear that is blocking your path, 'Look! I need to finish this. I need to finish this right now! Get out of my way!'

To which it responds, 'But look at aaalllll the time you've waaaasted. You'll never come back from this'.

You're frustrated so you push harder. 'It's your fault I'm so behind! I have to do three days' worth of work in one. So, get out of my way already!'

'If you were better, you wouldn't have spent all that time moping around on YouTube'.

'I know, okay? But if I don't do something I'm dead'.

'Why are you so out of control? It looks really bad. You know everyone thinks you're a joke'.

'Shit. Well, this is my last chance to prove them wrong, isn't it? I have to make this perfect. Move!'

'Perfect, in one day and with your track record? GF please'.

You tried to fight fear at its own game, and you lost. You can't belittle fear, you can't call fear names, and you can't yell at it. Because who you are really yelling at is you. Expressing anger or frustration shows fear that it's already won. Fear feeds on the negative tension you put out, making fear stronger and you weaker. It will trick you into agreeing that you're weak and helpless. Soon you will be doing its arguing for it. You can't out-fear the fear that stands between you and your dreams by coming down to its level. To dissolve it you must learn to speak the language of love.

Have you noticed the way toddlers verbalise every thought they have? The little chatterboxes explain everything: 'I put toy over there. I'll get it now. There it is. I found it'. Humans learn to think by speaking their thoughts aloud. As we get older and more socially aware, the dialogue becomes internal. The older we get the less we notice the internal chatter. When faced with a new challenge though, you will see yourself revert back to speaking your way through it. When driving to an unfamiliar place, I start to say things like, 'I need to turn right soon', 'No not Smith Street, James Street. Yes! That's the one'. Without realizing it, we talk to ourselves through every second of our lives. These internal conversations are our self-talk.

Self-talk can work for us or against us, so it's important to tune in to hear what it's saying. Keep a notebook or journal nearby as you go about your work. Listen for anything that pops up. It is usually when you hit an obstacle that you will catch it. It might say, 'God, nothing is ever simple'. Write it down. Don't think about it too much; just keep going. When I started watching what I was saying to myself, I quickly saw how belittling it was. 'I'm such an idiot', 'I'm not cut out for this', 'This will never work out' and on it goes, on repeat all day. How would you cope if you had someone sitting next to you saying such things? How productive would you be? Would you put up with it, or would you tell the person to get lost?

When we are unaware of the destructive and limiting things that we tell ourselves all day every day, we are unable to challenge them. Our subconscious accepts them, and they affect how we view the situation. Maybe you think you hate your job because your boss doesn't respect you when, in reality, there is a record playing in your head that tells you you're not good enough, and you don't matter. This record changes the way you present yourself at work and how you perceive your interactions with your boss. Listen up; it's time to take your power back.

WARNING: Be kind with yourself as you listen. Judging yourself for having negative thoughts and making yourself out to be a cruel or bitter person for thinking this way is not helping the situation. Criticism cannot end criticism; only kindness can. Accept yourself unconditionally.

REFLECTION

Document: Keep a notepad nearby as you work on your creative projects. Listen for your inner self-talk, and the things you say out loud. What kinds of conversations are you having with yourself?

Review: Read over these inner conversations like a witness. This can be painful. You may feel angry with yourself for being so hard on yourself. Doubts may creep in, such as, 'If this is what I think of myself, what must others think?' Detach yourself from your ego as much as you can.

Dispute: Are these comments true? If you heard someone say this to a friend of yours, how would you react? Are there holes in the logic? Does it sound like your voice or someone else's? A teacher, parent or bully perhaps? Where do you think these thoughts came from? To get to the root of the thoughts, ask your inner critic 'Why?' repeatedly until you get an answer. For me this exercise revealed my core belief was 'I can't'. For no logical reason I believed 'I can't'.

Replace: What are some more factual and helpful things you would say to yourself when obstacles arise? I clearly needed a big dose of self-belief. I would tell myself, 'I can! Look how far I've come! Of course I can!'

Discuss: If you allow your self-talk to go on uncensored, what sort of damage is it doing?

Replacing your negative self-talk with a positive affirmation can change your life if you let it. Author Louise Hay likens affirmations to seeds we plant for the reality we want to grow. Like a plant, affirmations do not bear fruit overnight. They need fertile soil (a peaceful mind) and consistent watering (daily repetition and action). Don't be deterred if they don't feel true at first. It has taken you decades to establish your negative thought patterns. It will take time to dismantle them and for new ones to stick. Popular affirmations are 'I love and approve of myself', 'I accept myself as I am' and 'All is well'. To prescribe yourself the most effective affirmation for your problem, you need to access your symptoms and look for the cause. This is why asking yourself why repeatedly (at least five times) is so important to get to the core of the belief and then tell yourself the exact opposite. Saying 'I feel' rather than 'I am' is another trick to make the affirmation feel more real.

I am weak.	I feel strong.
I hate myself.	I feel loved.

If it is still too difficult to say something positive about yourself, try saying your original negative thought in past tense (e.g., 'I used to think I was weak'), and be open to the possibility of change.

Positive affirmations can feel empty on their own. Your subconscious is not going to believe you if you say, 'I feel happy', when you say it with a sad facial expression and body language and then isolate yourself in a dark room for the rest of the day. To prove that you believe it, you must act it out. A great way to do this is to add a question at the end of your affirmation (e.g., 'What can I do to make you happy today?' or 'What do I need to feel happy today?'). Again this is about small steps as you move toward your desired feelings. Your action can be as tiny as a smile.

TIP: Say your affirmations in front of the mirror! Originally, I thought it was enough to repeat my affirmation three times a day. But when you realize your negative self-talk rarely stops to take a breath, three affirmations hardly seem like enough to make a difference. Now I use my mala beads, or any beaded necklace, to slide through my fingers and affirm something positive on each bead (which works out to be over one hundred affirmations). Louise Hay says two hundred is barely enough, which can seem like quite a time commitment. I like to work it into repetitive, mundane tasks like climbing stairs or doing the dishes. I did a six hour hike through Samaria Gorge once and when I wanted to give up I would repeat in my head, on every step, 'I am fit, fabulous and free'. Now, without thinking, every time I climb stairs I hear in my head 'I'm fit, fabulous and free'. If you repeat it enough, it will stick.

Inside Out is a gorgeous children's movie that illustrates the danger of replacing negative thoughts without hearing them out. In the movie the emotions of a girl are shown as characters called Joy, Sadness and so on. While Joy appears to be the hero, sadness is painted as the 'bad guy'. Thinking that we need to be happy all the time is misguided. Children are good role models in this regard, they don't hold back when they are sad; they let it out and then quickly move on. When a negative emotion is ignored, on the other hand, it knocks and knocks on your door, getting louder and louder. Its knocking can consume your life until it eventually kicks down the door and expresses itself. This is what happens in the movie. When sadness is finally allowed to come forth, it's cleansing and healing and not the disaster everyone anticipated. When you replace a negative thought that is still raw, remember that you have to 'feel it to heal it'. Let yourself feel your emotions fully and then move on.

As you become increasingly aware of your mind, you will find it has a sort of Tourettes Syndrome. Incorrect, inappropriate thoughts that you would never consciously think fly out of you all of the time. Things like 'she's fat'. When you catch them, it's impossible to take them back. The easiest way to forgive yourself for thinking it and releasing the negativity is to affirm 'I love you'. Love yourself, the thought and send love to the victim of the mean thought if there is one. Love is the answer to most things. The ancient Hawaiians knew this. Their spiritual practice of Ho'oponopono teaches us to accept radical responsibility for our entire reality and 'clean' the areas we want to improve. You clean by repeating 'I love you. I'm sorry. Please forgive me. Thank you'. Next time you're struggling to release something, I invite you to try it.

WARNING: When you start to disturb your deep, dark beliefs, like cleaning anything, it can get worse before it gets better. If you find things getting worse after you start working on your core negative beliefs, rest assured it means it's working. Be grateful for the discomfort; see it as progress. The following poem by Rumi explains the process perfectly.

This being human is a guest house.

Every morning a new arrival.

A joy, a depression, a meanness,

some momentary awareness comes

as an unexpected visitor.

Welcome and entertain them all!

Even if they are a crowd of sorrows,

who violently sweep your house

empty of its furniture,

still, treat each guest honorably.

He may be clearing you out

for some new delight.

The dark thought, the shame, the malice.

meet them at the door laughing and invite them in.

Be grateful for whatever comes.

because each has been sent

as a guide from beyond.

— Jellaludin Rumi,

translation by Coleman Bark

WATCH YOUR LANGUAGE

On your journey to becoming vibrantly creative and failure friendly, you need to release the negative self-talk that has been holding you back. Use the following table as a guide. Drop the apologetic victim phrases in the left column for the proactive and empowering phrases in the right.

Transform Your Language. Transform Your Mind	
>>>>>>>>>>>>>>>>>>>>>>>>>>>>>>>>>	
This is a mistake/failure.	This is a discovery.
I mucked up . . .	I learned that . . .
It's wrong.	It's interesting because . . .
I need to/have to . . .	I can . . .
I should . . .	I'm allowed to . . .
I can't . . .	How can I?
I'm scared/nervous/anxious about . . .	I'm excited about . . .
I don't know . . .	I'm curious about . . .
I'm not happy about . . .	Wouldn't it be great if . . .
I'm struggling.	I'm learning that . . .
I'm scared/uneasy.	I'm ready.
I don't have enough time.	Time is on my side.
There's too much to do.	I have come so far; my life is so full.
I don't know what to do.	I will know what to do when it feels right.
I can't deal with . . .	I can surrender to the free fall.
I don't have the answers.	Clarity comes from engagement.
I don't know what to do.	I will know what to do.
I don't know how to choose.	I choose to be calm and confident.
I don't know if I have what it takes.	I can do anything.
This is proof that I'm a failure/inadequate.	This is proof that I'm daring, learning and growing!

I feel nervous.	I feel butterflies in my tummy. I'm ready!
I want to give up.	I am being tested, I am getting stronger.
I'm stressed/overwhelmed.	I need a break or some me-time.
I'm sick of this.	How can I spice this up?
What if I fail?	No matter what I will be alright.
What will they think of me?	I accept myself no matter what.
I'm a fraud.	I love learning new skills.
I've already failed.	It's never too late.
I've wasted so much time.	One small step I can take right now is...
I don't know what to do.	I don't know what to do yet.
I'm so worried.	I'm ready to back myself.
This is hard.	This is living life outside of the comfort zone, baby!
Who am I to do this?	Who am I not to do this?
I just can't get started.	Why am I resisting?
The world is against me.	The universe supports me.
This is going to be too hard.	This might be easier than I thought.
I might not have what it takes.	I've gotten through worse.
There's so much to do.	I have come so far.
I don't know!	I love challenges!
I've never done this before.	I am living my dreams.
This is too big for me.	How can I break this down so it's manageable?
I am alone in this.	Who can I ask for help?
It's too risky.	Am I willing to fail in order to succeed?
It should be perfect.	My best is enough.
No one has faith in me.	I have faith in me because . . .

FRIEND – LOVE YOUR FEAR

Dealing with your negative self-talk lovingly as it arises is empowering. It can have lasting effects if you continue to work on your core limiting beliefs. But after a while, you will start to notice the same voices with the same concerns popping up time after time. These are not just passing thoughts; they are your ghosts. Ghosts are deep-seated characters that live in your head. They have one job and that's to protect you. They've been with you since you were about seven years old, since a time when you felt threatened in some way. They promised that little you that they would stay with you and keep you from feeling that way ever again. Heart-warming, yes, but is it wise to live your adult life based on the logic of a seven-year-old? Could it be that the interpretations and meaning you made back then, even though it was the best you could do with your level of consciousness, are not accurate or helpful now? I told my story at the beginning of this book. I was faced with a situation where I wasn't as good at reading or spelling as everyone else in my class. The best meaning I could come up with back then was that I wasn't as good as everyone else. As an adult I look back at that little me, and my heart breaks. She was perfect. She had a special gift for learning and communicating in a visual way, but she couldn't see it. If only she knew that in the future her skills in visual communication would be more valuable than ever. But she did her best. She created protectors that would guard her from the painful feelings of failure, of not being good enough. That's why they appear every time I am about to step into the spotlight or into a challenge where I may not succeed. My desire to live without regrets does not compute in the ghosts' minds because they have one role and one thought: protect.

Fear loves you. Love it back by listening to what it has to say and thanking it for sharing its concerns. When you see it as the scared little you that is trying to help, there is no need to get angry and no need to fight. Just smile at it, say, 'Thank you, but I promise we are safe; we can do this', then hold out your hand and step into uncertainty together. We all have friends who do things that can seem abrasive or inappropriate, but we keep them around anyway because their hearts are in the right place. Your ghost is that friend.

ACTION

It can be cleansing to write a letter to your younger self and your ghosts to thank them for all of their care. Apologise for not understanding them, and explain why they can now relax.

To befriend your ghosts, you need to get to know them. By continually tuning into your self-talk, you will start to notice the patterns. Put on your detective hat again, and track those patterns. Whose voices are they? What do they remind you of? Another approach is to take your list of failures, or write a one-page summary of your life. Read through it objectively or with a close friend to identify the patterns that jump out at you.

REFLECTION

What do I most commonly tell myself? Why?

What sort of activities trigger my ghosts? Why?

Did I experience anything traumatic as a child?

Whose voice do I hear when I'm in a state of uncertainty? Could it be a teacher or a parent? Why?

What are the recurring themes in my life? Why?

Have I repeated the same mistakes? Why?

What was I like as a child? How has that influenced who I am today?

What labels did I have in primary school and high school? How have those labels influenced who I am today? Why?
What am I most afraid of? Why?

NAME AND TAME IT

As you get to know the ghosts that haunt your mind, give them names, personalities and even outfits (the less scary the better). Create characters that are memorable for you. When they start to chatter, you can speak to them directly and calm them down ASAP. Naming and calling out your fears (some people call this 'naming and shaming', but there is no shame in the Failure Friendly mindset) is proven to calm the racing amygdala. The amygdala is deep in your brain. It's extremely powerful because it's been a part of the human brain forever. It kept our ancestors safe from predators, and as we've evolved it's only grown stronger. This fear is then fuelled by the right side of the brain, which deals with emotions. That's more than half of your brain on 'fear alert'. By using language, through writing or speaking, you engage the left and logical side of your brain. Logic and rational thinking have been paused during the 'fear alert', so it's important to jump start it back into action to get a grip on your mind.

I discovered that I have three ghosts, all tied into my core fear of 'not being good enough'. Interestingly, they resemble warped interpretations of my dad, my mum and my younger self. Let me introduce you to them.

Mr Whip	The Pusher	The Brat
He stands with his arms crossed and lays down the law or 'cracks the whip'. He is often found moving goalposts farther out of reach, and his only emotion is disappointment.	She is impatient and shrill. She enforces the law set by Mr Whip. Posing as the good cop, she pleads and then demands that things be done now! When progress is too slow, she can become very cruel.	This little ghost can stop the show by throwing a tantrum when she doesn't feel like anyone has her best interest at heart. She puts her foot down as soon as the pressure gets too high.

I've come to understand the relationships at play in this triangle of fear. Mr Whip sets the course, the Pusher does anything to keep Mr Whip happy and the Brat screams 'Stop!' when she's had enough. They all feed off each other, resulting in total dysfunction. But their hearts are in the right place. Now that I know my ghosts like I know the back of my hand, they rarely creep up on me. I can predict their outbursts and prepare them with a pep talk before they have to cause a fuss to get my attention, which works better for all of us.

REFLECTION

Who are the ghosts that haunt your mind? Give each one a name.

What are their personalities like?

What do they look like?

Who would play them in a movie?

What does each ghost need to hear to relax?

LEAD

Imagine a friend of yours is grappling with alcoholism. As their friend, should you enable them to continue drinking because that's what they want? Or should you refrain from aiding the addiction, allowing them to face the consequences of their actions, and support them while they learn the difficult lessons they require to heal? When you befriend your ghosts and fears, you may develop fondness for them and feel compelled to protect them from pain. But are you really protecting them by depriving them of the experiences that will make them stronger?

When you stop living small and start chasing big dreams, you invite bigger risks and a new level of uncertainty into your life. It's equally terrifying and rewarding. As I got into a regular habit of checking in with my ghosts, I began to resent the big risks I was taking. I saw only sacrifices and heavy burdens. I would say, 'My business has exploded', as if it had combusted instead of being excited about the growth and success. It was as if my ghosts had hit a plateau, a level of risk they were comfortable with, and refused to go any further. As their friend, I accepted this.

But my businesses continued to grow. They required new challenges like outsourcing and staffing to keep up with the demand, but the ghosts had drawn their line. I was torn. None of my strategies could penetrate the problem because I didn't know what it was. I just knew something was missing. So, I surrendered the problem to the universe and took a break. During the break I watched a pirate TV series called *Black Sails*. I was immediately hooked on the show. Possibly because I've always had an affinity with pirates, but it was more than that. I became inspired, tapping into that higher energy and came alive as I watched. In the show was the guidance I had requested and the lesson I needed to learn.

Our minds are like ships with the capabilities to take us on adventures anywhere we want to go. From the series, I leaned some of the sailing essentials, such as:

- You need a purpose as your compass to keep you on course.

- Let the present moment be your anchor.

- Focus on the journey rather than the destination.

- A smooth sea never made a skilled sailor.

My mind, however, was a ghost ship run by a dysfunctional trio of ghosts who refused to lose sight of the shore. We were doomed to float in the comfort zone because we had no captain and no crew. A captain's job is to have a clear vision that is bigger than the current voyage and dripping with purpose. It is the captain's job to lead the crew with an unshakeable faith and certainty. The captain must model bravery as the ship faces rough seas. The captain's conviction puts the crew at ease. The captain has a first mate or quartermaster, who is the go-between. He champions the captain's vision and eradicates doubts within the crew. He also reports back to the captain regarding the crew's needs and concerns. He is a storyteller who makes the captain's vision real in the hearts and minds of the crew. The crew are passionate about being part of a team and taking action. Life at sea is not for the faint hearted, so you must choose your crew wisely. There is no room for naysayers or big egos. The crew is strongest when they work as one. They rely on their captain and quartermaster for courage and direction. There is no stopping a ship that has a strong captain, a faithful quartermaster and a passionate crew, even if a few ghosts have stowed away on board.

So, how do we find our inner captain? Look to the leaders who have inspired you throughout history and in your own life. Find out as much as you can about them by reading books, watching movies and asking questions. Ask yourself what characteristics you admire most about them and why. What are their patterns of behaviour? How do they face uncertainty? Do you see any commonalities between them?

REFLECTION

Which leaders inspire you the most? List as many as you can.

What is it about these leaders that resonates with you?

What do these leaders have in common?

For me, I looked toward entrepreneurs and global change makers for inspiration. I became obsessed with leadership and read a lot of leader autobiographies. I found that the things they all had in common include the following.

- They didn't try to do it alone.

- They were aware of their own weakness and found people who could complement their strengths.

- They treated their teams with utmost respect, never bullying or pushing them to do anything they wouldn't do themselves. Instead, they empowered them with trust and responsibility.

- They inspired their teams by making sure everyone knew why they were chasing their goals.

All great leaders had a strong sense of purpose, to serve the world rather than themselves. Leaders are human and experience doubt and worry like all of us, but leaders know not to feed their worries or share them with their team. Their job is to be the beacon of hope. Leaders are told they are crazy, a lot. To everyone else their goals seem impossible, which makes leaders more determined to prove other people wrong. They face extreme ups and downs, and the one thing that gets through it is faith in their vision. Leaders are able to face the responsibility, the obstacles, the uncertainty and the naysayers because they truly believe they can do it. Self-belief is a choice they make every day.

As always, it makes sense in hindsight. By regularly checking in with the ghosts, I had focused on my fear. As the Law of Attraction says, 'What you focus on grows'. I had homed in on fear and forgotten about faith. To become the captain I needed to be, I had to shift my focus and accept that faith is not blind; it's visionary.

Write a letter from your future self as if your dream has already materialized. Visualise it coming true every morning when you wake up and every night before you go to sleep. Make your vision real by activating your senses, what does it feel like, look like, sound like, smell like, taste like? The crazy thing is your mind doesn't know it isn't real, experiencing a crystal clear vision has the same positive effect on the mind as remembering a time you overcame something similar. Protect your dream from naysayers, and join a community of people who choose to dare greatly with you. Commit to believing in yourself and your vision. Have unshakable and unapologetic faith in yourself, your creativity, your strength, your softness, your worth, your right to sit at the table, your ability to turn obstacles into opportunities, your skill to navigate through the storms, your courage to face of your fears, your resilience, your vision, your higher power and your ability to lead your ship to your dream life.

Let your faith be greater than your fear.

ACTION

As you continue to check in on your ghosts, check in with your captain and his or her or their vision, and review the needs of your quartermaster and your crew. Give them the direction they need. Paint them a word picture full of juicy details that activate their senses, record them a guided visualisation, make them a vision board, write them a visionary manifesto, chant for them your vision in slogan form.

OVER TO YOU

To worry is to bet against yourself. To challenge yourself is to back yourself. Set a creative challenge now, and commit to it. Make the lessons in this book real by putting them to the test. What scares you? Do that. When you rise to the challenge, you will surprise yourself, and my god, it is worth it! As I type the last few words of this book, I am filled with the feeling that I want you to experience: achievement. Confidence and satisfaction pump through me as I think, *If I can do this, what else can I do?* Having achievements behind you, no matter how small or great, will keep you going. When you hit the barriers, knowing you've been tested before, you can call on those previous triumphs and power on. I love challenges!

CHALLENGE

I challenge myself to:

Why am I challenging myself?

Am I willing to fail?

What will success look like?

What will failure look like?

What can I do to support myself?

How will I keep my vision and faith strong?

What sort of team do I need? How will I find them?

> How will I face my ghosts, my ego and other obstacles and mistakes as they arise?
>
> What past experience can I call on to help me?
>
> How do I want to feel on this journey?
>
> How will I know I have succeeded?
>
> How will I celebrate?
>
> Why am I accepting this challenge?
>
> What is the smallest step I can take right now?

On your creative quest, remember that the Failure Friendly Mindset is a tool you can call on at any time, with three ingredients that you can be used in any order:

Wake Up - Self-awareness in the moment (What am I thinking?)

Shake Up - Positive self-belief (What do I choose to think instead?)

Make Up - Unconditional self-compassion (How do I feel?)

And, Go - Rise to the challenge (I've got this!)

Remember that all of the tools, activities and reflections in this book, plus some bonus lessons on how to become a leader and lead your most creative life, can be downloaded and printed from www.failurefriendly.com

As this book ends, may it be a new beginning. Let's go!

ABOUT THE AUTHOR

Buzzy Lewis loves creativity. It lights her up, and it's how she pays the bills. She's been a graphic designer, marketing manager, artist, art teacher, entrepreneur and strategist.

But it's the dark side of creativity that led her to become a writer. Creative anxiety, self-doubt and creative burnout have tormented her, sucked all of her energy and left her for dead, forced her to look inside of herself, find resilience and grow into a better, stronger, calmer and more confident creative person. Researching and writing about the lessons from the dark-side of creativity became her obsession.

It was in 2016 during a particularly heavy bout of creative burnout, stuck in bed, Buzzy began to look through and organise the little notes she had written to herself about overcoming the fear of failure. Those notes quickly became the body of work that you now hold in your hands. The process of putting everything she had learned into one place helped to heal her wounds from years of chronic self-criticism. This is a book for healing.

It wasn't until the lockdown of 2020-21 that Buzzy remembered this little body of work and set about self-publishing it, but a lot had changed in five years. Her research had taken a shift, she had uncovered new metaphysical insights that go beyond what is covered in this book. That is how 'Being Creative', a visual book exploring the energetics of creativity, was written by Buzzy in less than a month and then published in late 2021, you can find a copy of it at www.failurefriendly.com

It's 2023 now, and it's time to release the original lessons that made so much creativity possible. Buzzy's wish is that:

"This collection of little pep-talks helps another fallen creative to lift themselves back up."

buzzy@failurefriendly.com

@failure_friendly

www.failurefriendly.com

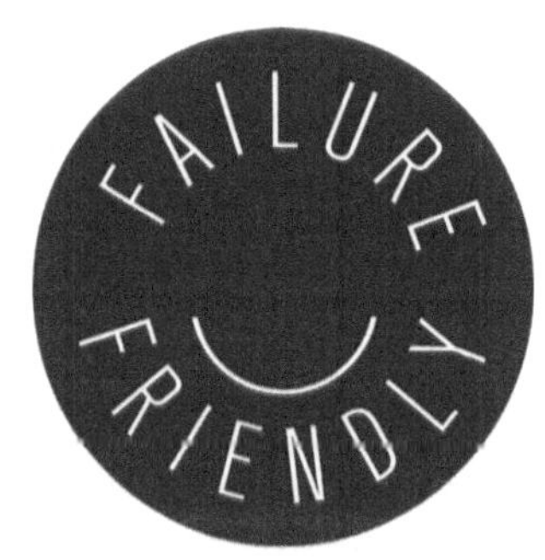

www.ingramcontent.com/pod-product-compliance
Lightning Source LLC
Chambersburg PA
CBHW031312060726
47590CB00003B/1174